The Parish Life Coordinator

An
Institute for Pastoral Life Study

Gary P. Burkart, Ph.D.

Sheed & Ward

Sheed & Ward™ is a service of The National Catholic Reporter Publishing Company.

Library of Congress Cataloguing in Publication Data

Burkart, Gary P., 1943-
    The parish life coordinator : an Institute for Pastoral Life study / Gary P. Burkart.
        p.   cm.
    Includes bibliographical references.
    ISBN: 1-55612-569-0 (alk. paper)
    1. Parish life coordinators. I. Institute for Pastoral Life.
II. Title.
BX1916.B87   1992
253--dc20   92-26970
                                                                  CIP

Published by: Sheed & Ward
                            115 E. Armour Blvd.
                            P.O. Box 419492
                            Kansas City, MO 64141-6492

To order, call: (800) 333-7373

Contents

Preface

In the following six chapters we will tell the story of the parish life coordinator using the social scientific perspective of the survey. We will relay large amounts of data collected in a representative fashion from PLCs, dioceses and parishioners in order to substantiate generalizations we have made concerning this model of lay ministry as it has evolved since the early 1980s.

In way of a preface, we emphasize that ours is not a study that attempts to wrestle with or solve the many delicate theological issues raised by the PLC model. Our expertise lies only in the social science field. Accordingly, we have found data indicating that the PLC approach is meeting contemporary needs of parishes, parishioners and dioceses in an era of priest shortage. Likewise we have found data indicating that this approach leaves continuing difficulties. It is not our position to make definitive statements about the overall worth of the PLC model. Our study does reveal, however, that Catholic parishioners in the U.S. are overwhelmingly accepting of this approach when they see that a need exists. We have uncovered abundant evidence that lay people see expanded lay roles in their parishes as appropriate and many are interested themselves and are willing to be trained to take on these roles. The laity in parishes with and without PLCs are accepting and would accept a PLC "solution" to the priest shortage. Others in the Church will have to evaluate the relative merits and weaknesses of other approaches, such as consolidation of parishes and multiparish priests, as responses to the same situation. That which follows, then, is the first comprehensive, empirical look at the phenomenon of the parish life coordinator from the vantage points of the PLCs themselves, their parishioners and their dioceses.

Organization of the Book

Chapter 1 presents the scope and methods of our empirical study of PLCs. The study was planned with a practical bent to it; these data were collected primarily to aid the Institute for Pastoral Life in its work of formation of the PLC. Findings will be used to guide policy formation and implementation over the coming years. We conceived of our study in broad terms as well; not only were PLCs studied but also their parish and diocesan contexts. Chapter 1 relays the main social science methodologies used to realize these goals. The techniques employed to define the PLC, diocesan and parishioner samples are explained as well as the derivation of the five research instruments used with the various samples. The contents of the instruments are herein presented in abbreviated form. Finally, we give a cursory discussion of our data analysis techniques.

Chapter 2 presents findings concerning the core of our study—the parish life coordinator. We first outline the perceptions that PLCs have of any existing policies concerning their position as promulgated by either their diocese or their parish. Not only do we measure the perceptions that PLCs have about eleven specific policies, but we also probe these ministers' sense of the adequacy of these policies. Our data indicate that the absence (and inadequacy) of PLC policies has a large negative effect upon (1) PLC emotional states, (2) relations with the sacramental minister and the canonical pastor and (3) the degree of ambiguity the PLC feels in her* role as PLC of a parish.

Chapter 2 also presents data on the PLC's perceptions of the adequacy of both diocesan and parish planning for parish life coordination as well as her own planning and formation for the PLC position. We were guided by the belief that if the PLC perceives planning to be inadequate, she will likewise feel that PLC polices, either at the diocesan or parish levels, are

---

* As 86 percent of the PLC sample was female, we use the femine form to describe the PLC throughout this book.

absent or inadequate. It is quite likely that the sensing of inadequate PLC planning will also be related to (1) a feeling of ambiguity in her PLC role and (2) the emotional states she experiences.

Finally this chapter takes a closer look at how much ambiguity the PLC experiences in her role: (1) the origins of role ambiguity in inadequate PLC policies and PLC planning at the diocesan and parish levels, (2) the impact of this ambiguity on impaired relations with those with whom the PLC associates and (3) ambiguity's impact upon her emotional status.

Chapter 3 is a comparison between the dioceses in our sample that now have PLCs with those dioceses which might adopt PLCs in the near future. We present data on the use of PLCs by these dioceses as well as any future intent to use the PLC by those dioceses not now deploying them. For those dioceses with PLCs we explore the process of selecting, training and placing of the PLC. We conclude by looking at the diocesan planning process for PLCs, the components of the diocesan PLC policy, what is working and not working with the PLC model and any alternative models to the PLC that the diocese may anticipate.

Chapter 4 introduces the findings of our study based on the responses from parishioners with parish life coordinators. We present data on how evaluations of the PLC are made by parishioners. In particular we investigate diocesan, parish and parishioner factors that affect the degree of acceptance of the PLC by her parishioners. In addition we offer findings that reveal that a high percentage of these parishioners are open to nonpriests as "pastors" in the event their parish would not have a full-time priest available. Finally, we will elaborate on data that show that parishioners with PLCs view nontraditional roles for laity (such as giving homilies, conducting certain services, preparing fellow parishioners sacramentally) as appropriate for lay persons like themselves. Furthermore we discover that high percentages are interested in these roles for themselves and say that they would be willing to be trained for the roles if such services were available.

Chapter 5 presents the findings from the sample of parishioners who do not now have PLCs in their parishes but who may have them in the near future. We were most interested in these parishioners' attitudes concerning the possibility of a part-time priest and a PLC in their parish in the near future. We were also interested in whether they had experienced the lack of a full-time priest in their parish at some point in the past, and whether they were aware of any diocesan plan to assign a part-time priest in the future. We not only present data on these questions in Chapter 5 but again, as in the sample of parishioners with PLCs, we produce information revealing that many of these parishioners would be willing to accept a nonpriest as their "pastor" in the event their parish would not have a full-time priest available. Finally, we will elaborate on data that show that parishioners with PLCs view nontraditional roles for laity (such as giving homilies, conducting certain services, preparing fellow parishioners sacramentally) as appropriate for lay persons like themselves. Furthermore we discover that high percentages are interested in these roles for themselves and say that they would be willing to be trained for the roles is such services were available.

Chapter 6 presents conclusions to our main findings of the five samples in the form of generalizations. We then state some implications of these generalizations for policy-makers at the diocesan and parish levels. The chapter ends with a section on what is and isn't working with the PLC model from three different perspectives: the PLC's, the dioceses, and the parishes that have PLCs.

No project of the scope of this study could be done without much assistance and help. The Institute for Pastoral Life, until recently headquartered in Kansas City, Missouri, should be credited with perceiving the need for a firm data base upon which to do future planning and development by commissioning this project. Furthermore, without the funding of the Raskob Foundation, such a large study could not have been possible. The gentle leadership provided by the Director of IPL, Jean Marie Hiesberger, made my job as project director such a pleasure. I am most grateful to Fr. Phil Murnion of the National Pastoral Life Center in New York City and Dr. Ruth Wallace of George Washington University in Washington, D.C. for their reading and suggestions for the research instruments used in this investigation. My research assistants, Mary Randall, Shannon Burkart, Meredith Allen, Michele Saladrigas and

Preface / ix

Dana Lomshek made the jobs of mailing questionnaires, coding, and data entry so efficient and organized for me.

I am immensely grateful to a reaction group that was assembled to help me with interpretations of findings from the study's data. The group consisted of Ms. Jean Marie Hiesberger, Mr. Robert Heyer, Editor-in-Chief of Sheed and Ward, Bishop Sullivan of the St. Joseph-Kansas City Diocese in Missouri, and four Parish Life Coordinators—Michele Fehr, Sr. Jay McCann, SHJC, Margaret Lima, and Sr. Helen Walling, IHM. Their insights into the generalizations produced by our research have been incorporated into the book in a number of spots. Of course, a huge debt of gratitude exists with the many Parish Life Coordinators, dioceses, bishops, and diocesan functionaries, parish priests and parishioners who made this study possible by the donation of their time and concern during the data gathering stage of the research. I can only hope that I have adequately told their many stories. Without the acceptance of the validity of this project's work by Bob Heyer, Editor of Sheed and Ward, this book would never have been published and without the interest from the readers who bought this book, our findings would never have been disseminated in such a widespread manner. Special thanks and recognition is extended to my Social Research classes of the past two years who helped me review the literature on the phenomenon of the Parish Life Coordinator.

A word of thanks goes to all of my colleagues in the Sociology department at Benedictine College, my other colleagues and administrators at the college, and my students who hopefully excused me from this or that obligation because of a need to work on "the project." Finally, my appreciation goes to my wife Eileen, and my children, Chris, Kelly, Shannon, Heather and Ryan who saw less of me than perhaps they needed or wanted due to a need to get on with the work of producing the first general study of the Parish Life Coordinator in the Catholic church in the United States.

Gary P. Burkart
Atchison, Kansas
May, 1992

1.

The Scope and Methods of the Institute for Pastoral Life's Study of Parish Life Coordinators

A. The Origins of the Study

During this evolutionary time in the American Catholic Church, the Institute for Pastoral Life in Kansas City has spearheaded the move to provide formation of lay ministers. Its particular focus has been the formation of the Parish Life Coordinator (PLC), a lay pastoral leadership role that has evolved out of the lay ministry movement in the post-Vatican II era. The revised Code of Canon Law (1983), acknowledging the need for pastoral supervision of parishes with part-time priests makes some provision for pastoral care by others than ordained priests. The Code left the exact nature of the position open and various models have evolved within contemporary American Catholicism.

It is often said that the faster an institution changes, the more careful must be its planning. With the world constantly changing in new and bewildering ways, the global Church finds itself in a state of chronic change and must carefully plan to bring its institutions into a continually evolving world. While many dioceses have struck upon the PLC role to help answer their current pastoral needs, shifting trends could see this evolutionary structure crumble at some point in the future. Any organization trying to meet the needs of the Church with this innovative form of pastoral care should base its planning and policy on sound empirical knowledge of the situation of the PLC, the parish in which the PLC ministers, and the diocese which gives it sponsorship.

In an attempt to anticipate and plan for change, the Institute, with the help of a grant from the Raskob Foundation, commissioned a comprehensive study of the Parish Life Coordinator. The study began in late spring 1990.

No one has ever studied empirically the Parish Life Coordinator model in depth. Peter Gilmore's[1] pioneering work, while rich in anecdotal materials and full of insights based on the actual experience of the first wave of emergent "lay pastors," was limited to a handful of cases. We have no studies of all the PLCs working in the American Church. Furthermore, while IPL has been working closely with most of the dioceses that have been using the PLC model, no global picture of the practices and policies of these dioceses exists. While it appears that a number of dioceses are about to adopt this form of pastoring to help solve their critical human resources needs, no composite of these dioceses exists and no comparisons exist between these dioceses and the more experienced dioceses that have been using PLCs for some years.

Likewise no one has measured the attitudes of parishioners who have experienced this new phenomenon, sometimes without knowing what was happening to them. Have these parishioners been in a state of shock? Are they rejecting these "lay pastors"? Are they willing to give them a try after a period of doubt? The most knowledge we have had before this present study has been anecdotal information of how parishioners are reacting to this new development in their religious lives.

Finally, we have had virtually no information of what parishioners about to lose their priest-pastor are thinking. Are they anticipating his departure with dread and denial? Could they accept someone other than an ordained priest to pastor their congregation? Are these parishioners at all willing to help take up the slack by receiving training to take on pastoring roles themselves in the absence of a resident priest?

Thus, the IPL Study was constructed to get a look at the big picture: What and who are the PLCs? How have and will dioceses support and develop the PLC model? What has been happening to parishioners in their parishes without full-time pastor-priests? Can parishioners in parishes that now have a resident priest but may not have one for long be adequately prepared to accept a parish without a resident priest and to accept one with a Parish Life Coordinator? These are some of the questions that our study has tried to answer.

The IPL Parish Life Coordinator Study should be seen as a part of a larger attempt to understand the contemporary growth in lay ministry. As such, IPL has cooperated with two other ongoing investigations into lay ministry within American Catholicism: that of Dr. Ruth Wallace of George Washington University in Washington, D.C., and that of the National Pastoral Life Center in New York City.

Dr. Wallace's study, funded by a grant from the Lilly Foundation, focused deeply on PLCs in the context of their parishes. She has traveled to these parishes and lived with each of the PLC's for a period of time. Her research mode is more that of a field study/participant observation design. In helping us to understand the PLC role from the inside and as it exists in the context of the parish, her investigation adds depth to the work of Gilmore.

The National Pastoral Life Center, using the research background with the Notre Dame Study of Catholic Parish Life, put together for the National Conference of Catholic Bishops a study of the whole of lay ministry. In this framework the PLC is just one lay ministry among many. After this study is complete we should have a better appreciation of where

Parish Life Coordinators fit into the diversity of lay ministries that have blossomed in recent years.

Our present study investigated the middle ground between the case study, in-depth approach of Wallace and the more global design of Murnion. Ours is the first national *survey* study of the PLC phenomenon. It is designed to study (1) the entire population of all PLCs in the U.S. Catholic Church, (2) a large representative sample of parishioners and (3) a pool of most of the dioceses in the country that either are using PLCs or may be using them in the near future. Added to the Wallace and NPLC research, this study should provide a comprehensive data set on contemporary PLCs.

B. The Samples Used in the Study

1. The PLC Sample

Our study was designed from its inception to include all persons doing the job of a Parish Life Coordinator in the United States. As the PLC is a relatively new phenomenon, the total number was believed to be manageable. Therefore no attempt was envisioned to sample from this group. While simplifying the sampling design, the problem arose immediately of determining whom should be considered a legitimate PLC and therefore placed in our population to be studied.

The approach finally settled upon was to use the best, updated list that IPL had from its contacts and operations. We will return to the question of definition shortly. When we cross-checked the IPL list with *The National Catholic Directory*, published by P. J. Kenedy & Sons, a number of discrepancies were found. Names that were on the IPL list were not in the Kenedy directory. Names in the directory were not on the IPL list. The IPL list contained a total of 147 names of those believed by IPL to be "doing Parish Life Coordinator work." The geographic distribution of these names is as follows:

Table 1.1
Geographic Distribution of PLCs
Who Responded to IPL Study
(Total=116)*

Northeast (2)
    Pennsylvania (1)
    New York (1)

Southeast (6)
    Georgia (2)
    North Carolina (3)
    Virginia (1)

South Central (24)
    Kentucky (8)
    Louisiana (4)
    Mississippi (3)
    Tennessee (9)

Mid-central (27)
    Indiana (2)
    Ohio (2)
    Michigan (17)
    Illinois (1)
    Wisconsin (5)

Midwest (28)
    Oklahoma (2)
    Missouri (5)
    Minnesota (7)
    South Dakota (2)
    North Dakota (2)
    Texas (10)

West (29)
    Alaska (7)   Utah (4)
    Arizona (3)   New Mexico (2)
    Colorado (1)   Wyoming (1)
    California (2)   Montana (2)
    Idaho (1)   Washington (5)
    Oregon (1)

* 102 returns were useable.

2. Dioceses with PLCs

The matter of selecting a sample of dioceses with PLCs was a relatively easy matter. Other than possible disagreements on definition, all that was needed was a list of dioceses known by IPL to be using PLCs. The IPL list contained 61 client dioceses at the time the sample was defined.

The geographic distribution of those dioceses that cooperated with our study and those PLCs who responded to this survey study are as follows:

Table 1.2
Geographic Distribution of IPL Client Dioceses in Return Sample

Northeast	3 Dioceses
Southeast	4 Dioceses
South Central	9 Dioceses
Mid-central	14 Dioceses
Midwest	14 Dioceses
West	12 Dioceses

Active priest/parish ratios and laity/active priest ratios were constructed for these and all other dioceses in the United States (see Table 1.3.) It will be noted that there is little difference on the laity/active priest ratio's between the dioceses with PLCs (1,332 laity per priest) and the set of general dioceses (1,339 laity per each priest). However, the ratio of 1,322 is significantly different from the 1,108 ratio for the dioceses without PLCs. This is the only indicator on which the dioceses with PLC's are significantly different from the dioceses without PLCs. These indicators demonstrate that the PLC dioceses and the dioceses without PLCs are very similar types of dioceses and are significantly different from the general set of dioceses.

3. Dioceses without PLCs

The task of picking a sample of dioceses without PLC's was more challenging. We did not want to take all dioceses in the U.S. but to study only those dioceses that may be adopting the PLC model in the next five years. It can be argued that the PLC movement is old enough and that we have learned enough that a second phase of development may be taking place for the newer set of dioceses that adopt this approach. We wanted to assemble a sample of these dioceses. First we included dioceses known by IPL to be moving toward adoption of the PLC. Additionally, we constructed another list of dioceses that exceeded certain cut-off points on two ratios that were computed for all dioceses in the U.S. These two ratios were the (1) active priest/parish ratio (Line 10 in Table 1.3)

Table 1.3
Priest/Parish/Laity Ratios

Characteristics of Diocese*	General	Dioceses With PLCs	Without PLCs
1. Priestless parishes (average number)	4.32	14.16	16.40
2. Parishes (average total number)	122	97	96
3. Total Catholics (average total number)	465,000	187,925	167,000
4. Total priests in diocese (average)	351	156	150
5. Religious priests (average)	159	62	54
6. Active diocesan priests (average)	190	94	95
7. Laity/active priest ratio (per priest)	1,339	1,332	1,108
8. Active priest/laity ratio (per 10,000 Laity)	09	10	11
9. Parishes/active priest (per parish)	.45	.78	.70
10. Active priests/parishes (per parish)	2.5	1.6	1.5
Total dioceses = 171	76	61	34

*Based on Kenedy Directory, 1991.

which consisted of the number of active priests in a diocese divided by the number of parishes in that same diocese and (2) the laity/active priest ratio (Line 7 in Table 1.3) which was constructed from the total number of Catholics in the dioceses divided by the number of active priests in the diocese.

After the ratios were constructed for all dioceses, these dioceses were plotted on a graph that had as its horizontal axis the laity/active priest ratio and as its vertical axis the active priest/parish ratio.

The dioceses with PLCs and the list of dioceses believed by IPL to be moving toward PLCs were then plotted on the graph and color-coded to the type of diocese. Based on these plots a further sample of dioceses that were physically close to the graph to the dioceses with PLCs and those thought by IPL to be near to adopting PLCs were chosen. It will be noted in the graph that the intersection of the two ratios (their averages for all dioceses in that group) for the dioceses with PLCs and the dioceses without PLCs are located close together. Whereas this intersection of the two ratios (their averages) for the dioceses in general is at a higher spot on the priest/parish ratio line. This graphically shows that the dioceses with PLCs and the dioceses without PLCs differ from the population of general dioceses on the active priest/parish ratio but not on the laity/active priest ratio. This again indicates that the dioceses

Graph 1.1
Data from "Ratios on Dioceses"

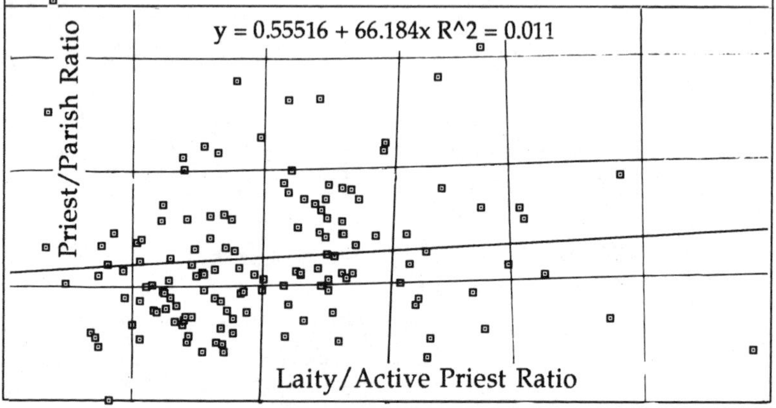

$y = 0.55516 + 66.184x \quad R^2 = 0.011$

Priest/Parish Ratio

Laity/Active Priest Ratio

with PLCs and dioceses without PLCs are similar kinds of dioceses and differ from the general dioceses. We therefore feel confident that the two samples of dioceses chosen are similar.

When the two sets of dioceses that resulted from these methods were added they totalled 34. The geographic distribution for those dioceses that cooperated with our study are included in the chart on the previous page.

4. Parishes with PLCs

To get a sample of parishioners with PLCs, the original list of PLCs was sampled systematically starting at random. A sampling interval was followed (every nth case chosen) to avoid entering any bias into the selection. More names were drawn than the total number sought so that if the one chosen could not cooperate another randomly drawn PLC could be contacted. A cover letter was then sent to the PLC asking for her to volunteer her parish for our study. She was asked to announce the selection of her parish to her congregation and to ask them to cooperate by filling out a questionnaire that would be mailed to them shortly. If the congregation cooperated, the PLC sent a parish roster. This roster was sampled systematically with a random start and a sampling interval was followed to select the number of participants for the study. If the parish list was small, usually under 60, all the names were contacted. If the parish was larger, anywhere from 40 to 70 parishioners were drawn systematically from the parish list. All names were drawn in such a way that they were representative of their parish.

Table 1.4
Dioceses in Final Sample
Which May Accept PLCs in Next 5 Years

Northeast	3 Dioceses
Southeast	3 Dioceses
South Central	2 Dioceses
Mid-central	2 Dioceses
Midwest	17 Dioceses
West	3 Dioceses

A total of 15 parish lists was received and 687 question-naires were sent to parishioners in these 15 parishes. The PLC's were promised summary results of their parishioner's responses at the end of the study. The geographic distribution of the parishes is as follows:

Table 1.5
Geographic Distribution of Parishes With PLCs

1.	South Central: Mississippi, Tennessee	2 Parishes
2.	Midwest: Minnesota, South Dakota, North Dakota, Arkansas, Missouri	8 Parishes
3.	Mid-central: Ohio, Michigan	4 Parishes
4.	West: Oregon	1 Parish

5. Parishes Without PLCs

The design to get a sample of parishioners in parishes without PLCs was more involved. Based on judgmental evidence of the Director of the Institute for Pastoral Life, a sample of bishops was chosen who were believed to be apt to implement the PLC model. The bishops were asked by mail or by telephone to name a parish in each of their dioceses that may be in jeopardy of losing its full-time priest within the next five years. The difficulty of making such a determination was appreciated by the research team, but if a sample was to be obtained of parishioners facing parish life without a resident priest, such information was necessary. When the bishop sent a name, the pastor was contacted and asked to cooperate with our study. Through a cover letter or a phone call, he was asked to volunteer his parish for study in light of his bishop's recommendation. He was asked to announce to his congregation that they would be receiving a questionnaire and a cover letter explaining the purpose of the study.

When the parish lists were received a systematic sample with a random start was made. Anywhere from 40 to 70 parishioners per parish were contacted. A total of 6 parishes cooperated, and 281 questionnaires were mailed to these parishes. The 6 parishes are geographically distributed as follows:

Table 1.6 Geographic Distribution of Parishes Without PLCs	
1. Midwest: Texas	2 Parishes
2. Mid-central: Michigan	2 Parishes
3. South Central: Mississippi	1 Parish
4. Mid-central: Ohio	1 Parish

C. Measurement Techniques

The fact that five different samples were studied necessitated a series of research instruments, one for each sample. Ideas for these instruments came from a wide variety of sources. Peter Gilmore's work was helpful in pointing out some of the sources of conflict and tension in this new structure of ministry. Another source of ideas was a questionnaire given to PLCs during the 1987 IPL Summer Institute in Kansas City, Missouri. Many areas that eventually went into the present instrument came from this source.[2]

Perhaps most instrumental in the derivation of items for these questionnaires was the experience gained in an 1989 Institute for Pastoral Life symposium entitled "Parish Leadership in Light of Diminishing Numbers of Priests." This symposium brought together a large group of bishops and diocesan officials to talk about PLC models. (cf. *Staffing Tomorrow's Parishes*, Maurice Monette.[3]) A further source of ideas came from another IPL conference on priest-PLC relations and its published proceedings, *Partners in Ministry: Priests in Collaboration with Parish Life Coordinators*.[4]

Finally, the experienced opinion of the IPL staff has lent credence to many of the items included in the instruments. Their insights from years of work with PLCs in the field were collected and incorporated in the research questions finally presented to the PLCs, the dioceses and the parishioners.

The items culled from these sources and experiences were then submitted to a three-level process of refinement. At each stage some combination of the project director, the IPL staff, Dr. Ruth Wallace and Fr. Phil Murnion passed judgment on the items and their phrasing. It is felt that a collective wisdom has been incorporated into the instruments.

The very nature of the Parish Life Coordinator phenomenon made measuring the concepts, variables, dimensions and indicators a difficult process. While every attempt was made to simplify and streamline the final items incorporated in the questionnaires, the very newness and unfamiliarity of the phenomenon made it difficult for some of the research subjects to know how to respond in all cases. While PLCs were familiar with this territory, some were doing work that perhaps would not qualify them as a PLC by the definition we used. Some of these therefore had difficulty deciding if the items on the questionnaire applied to them. The very fluidity of lay ministry also meant that while some were doing PLC work at the time they were placed on IPL's list, by the time they received our questionnaire, they had moved on to another job and/or setting.

To bring some consistency to the study, we had to settle on a definition of Parish Life Coordinator. The term itself is unclear both sociologically and theologically. The parish work to which the label of PLC is attached is called many things in many places and areas. Such persons are variously called pastoral associates, parish directors, pastoral administrators and parish administrators. To build some common ground, our study defined PLCs as *those persons who are appointed to the pastoring role in a parish in the absence of a resident priest.* As such a PLC would be the person who takes care of the pastoral supervision of the parish. The PLC would be the person who coordinates all the other ministries of the parish, such as education, outreach, administration, liturgy, music and enabling ministries. In effect it is doing, when no priest is available, all those things in a parish that do not require ordination. While Canon Law stipulates that only an ordained priest can be the pastor of a parish, PLCs are given day-to-day pastoral supervision by the bishop or some other ordained person. The Eucharist and the celebration of the Sacraments are taken care of by one or more priests who come into the parish part-time.

Thus, for the purposes of our study, a PLC is anyone appointed to the pastoral supervision of a parish in the absence of a resident priest. Parish administrators or pastoral associates would not be considered PLCs according to this definition, although those called pastoral administrators fit our definition. So that some consistency could result from sample to sample, all participants were presented with this one definition.

The following is a summary of the major areas that were studied in each of the research instruments (a different set went to each of the five samples).

1. The Parish Life Coordinator
    a. The role of diocesan, parish and PLC planning (formation)
    b. PLC policy (knowledge of its presence and adequacy to the PLC)
    c. Formation experiences of the PLC
    d. PLC emotions and needs
    e. Role relations of the PLC (affirming and non-affirming)
    f. Success and failure of the PLC
    g. Existence of role ambiguity in the PLC Role

2. Parishes without a Parish Life Coordinator
    a. Attitudes about who is qualified to pastor their parish
    b. Feelings about having a PLC with a part-time priest in the parish
    c. The appropriateness of certain roles for the laity
    d. Interest and willingness to be trained for these lay roles.

3. Parishes with a Parish Life Coordinator
    a. Attitudes about who is qualified to pastor their parish
    b. What roles are appropriate for lay persons
    c. Interest and willingness to be trained for these lay roles
    d. The parishioner's evaluation of the PLC

4. Dioceses with and without Parish Life Coordinators
   a. Use of PLCs in the dioceses
   b. Future Date at which PLCs will be used
   c. Settings in which PLCs are used
   d. Diocesan plans for picking parishes for PLCs
   e. The Diocesan PLC Planning process
   f. The Components of the diocesan PLC Policy formation, accountability, advertising, interviewing, hiring, contracting, installation, internships, diocesan affiliation of the PLC, financial assistance, appropriate activities for the PLC, evaluation of the PLC
   g. What is and is not working with PLCs in the diocese
   h. Diocesan alternatives to the PLC

As no previous social scientific research has been conducted on PLCs, no research instruments with measures of validity and reliability exist. Our instruments have not been tested for either of these, but because of the long process of deriving the items it is felt that these instruments have a validity at face value. To better measure the thoughts of those studied, a series of open-ended questions were incorporated with the other closed-ended items. While these present difficulties in coding and analyzing data, they present a wealth of information that could not be gathered in any other way.

D. Data Gathering

So that the samples would be as representative as possible of the populations from which they were drawn, a series of data-gathering steps were taken to insure as high a return as possible. We will describe these techniques below.

1. Dioceses

Each of the dioceses in the two different diocesan samples (with PLCs and without PLCs) were mailed a diocesan research instrument with a cover letter explaining the scope and purpose of the IPL study. They were asked for their cooperation and then promised confidentiality at the first phase of the research and anonymity at a later stage. To match questionnaires from PLCs and parishioners in their dioceses, a numerical code was placed on each of the questionnaires. Respondents were told that after an initial matching of the diocesan questionnaire with the PLC and parishioners in that diocese, the codes would be destroyed, thus depriving the research team of any knowledge of which dioceses responded or their particular answers. Additionally, each diocese was asked to send any documents they had put together that dealt with their diocese's position on the PLC. The data-gathering strategies resulted in a 93 percent return; 57 of the 61 dioceses with PLCs returned useable questionnaires. Likewise, 29 of the 34 dioceses without PLCs returned useable questionnaires, or an 85 percent return. Combining the samples, approximately 90 percent of the dioceses chosen for our study responded.

2. Parish Life Coordinators

In a similar fashion, the PLC's were sent cover letters and questionnaires. We received 116 responses, 14 of whom said that they no longer were doing pastoral administration work, that someone new had taken over the parish, or they were not reached by the postal service in time to cooperate. The remaining 102 useable questionnaires represented 70 percent of the original sample. Of these, 15 also volunteered their parishioners for an in-depth study of parishioner perceptions of the PLC.

3. Parishioners with and without PLCs

We used the same procedure for collecting data from parishioners. As the returns on all samples were high, we felt that this method was worth any inconvenience caused the respondents. A total of 968 parishioners were mailed cover letters and questionnaires. For the parishes without PLCs 282 questionnaires were sent and 183 (65 percent) responded. For the parishes with PLCs, 687 questionnaires were sent and 385 (56 percent) were received. Altogether, 568 of the 968 parishioner questionnaires were returned for a 59 percent overall return.

E. Data Analysis

The data from 102 PLCs, 86 dioceses (PLC and no PLC) and 568 parishioners (PLC and no PLC) were then coded and made ready for computer analysis. On most open-ended items three responses were coded. On those that promised more than three pieces of useful information in a respondent's open-ended answer, up to five responses were coded. After the results from these open-ended questions were printed out they were summarized so that only totals for each open-ended item are reported throughout this book.

Based on summary tables from the computer processing of the data, generalizations from the data were made. To help interpret generalizations and other study findings a reaction group was assembled comprised of four practicing PLCs, a bishop, the project director, the director of the Institute for Pastoral Life and the editor of Sheed & Ward. These comments were taped and incorporated into the generalizations and interpretations found in the text of this book.

Notes

1. Gilmore, Peter, *The Emergent Pastor* (Sheed & Ward), 1985.

2. Gallagher, Maureen, *Continuing the Journey: Parishes in Transition* (Sheed & Ward: Kansas City), 1988.

3. Monette, Staffing Tomorrow's Parishes (Sheed & Ward) 1990.

4. Monette, Maurice, *Partners in Ministry* (Sheed & Ward), 1989.

2.

Responses from Parish Life Coordinators

A. Areas of Investigation

The scope of the study of parish life coordinators was extensive. In general, we wanted to get a comprehensive understanding of the world of pastoral administration. We looked at samples of dioceses and parishes and sought to understand the relations between the parish life coordinator and the parish, deanery and diocese. In particular we wanted to investigate the relations between the PLC and the canonical pastor and the sacramental minister.

We first asked the PLCs to respond in two different ways on the questionnaires: one for their combined canonical pastor and sacramental minister and again for their sacramental minister if this person was different from the canonical pastor. For both of these individuals, we investigated positive and negative responses. Based on the suggestions found in Monette's *Staffing Tomorrow's Parishes*[1] we constructed examples of affirming relations—for example, does the canonical pastor and sacramental minister invite the PLC to take a visible leadership role at the liturgy and does he delegate to the PLC requests from parishioners that require decision-making? The PLCs were given a list of ten such possible relations. Furthermore, we presented the PLCs with a list of six possible nonaffirming relations with their canonical pastor and sacramental minister—for example, do you have uncomfortable feelings such as hurt, anger or fear in your dealings with them and are you treated in an unequal or discriminatory fashion? Through these questions we could get a comprehensive view of how the PLC relates to those with whom she must interact.

Second, we explored the social psychology of the PLC in terms of her needs and emotional states. PLCs were asked to state in an open-ended way what needs were being fulfilled and what needs were going unfulfilled in their job as PLC in the parish. The PLC was asked to identify with sixteen emotional states, such as "successful," "exhausted," "burned out," "frustrated," "well-received," "accomplished," "supported by the priests and bishop," and so on.

Third, we looked at the degree to which the PLC felt ambiguity in her role of PLC. We attempted to measure this ambiguity as it came from both the diocese and from the parish.

Finally, in addition to the relational and psychological states of the PLCs we measured how the PLCs felt about the outcome of their work in the parish. We asked them to talk about what was working and what was not working about ministering as PLCs in their parishes.

So the variables of role relations, psychological state, role ambiguity and role outcome became the main areas to be explained—the dependent variables—in the PLC sample. We went further in our design to try to uncover some of the correlates or causes--independent variables—of these four PLC conditions.

First, we correlated the dependent variables of role relations, etc., with the level of planning the PLC perceived to exist. We wanted to know how adequate the PLC felt diocesan, parish and her own planning or formation were for the PLC role. Second, we correlated the dependent variables with the PLC's perception of policy. We wanted to know first of all

if she perceived that PLC policies existed either in the diocese
or parish or in both, and then we wanted to know how adequate she felt these policies were. Eleven such policies were
presented to the PLCs for evaluation: for example, statements
relating the PLC to other ministries in the diocese, lines of accountability for the PLC in the parish and internship policies.

Next we proposed that the type of formation of the PLC
would act as an independent variable to the dependent variables. We measured not only the type of formation, formal or
informal, but also the level of adequacy of these formation experiences.

Finally, we tested as explanations for the dependent variables the requirements that PLCs had to meet to become a
PLC.

Thus we isolated four main causal factors, or independent variables: the level and adequacy of PLC *planning*, the existence and adequacy of PLC *policy*, the types of *formation*, and
the types of PLC *requirements* to work in the parish. These
four factors were then correlated in various ways to the dependent factors of role relations, psychological state, role ambiguity and role outcome of the PLC. The chart below presents
a visual picture of the PLC study.

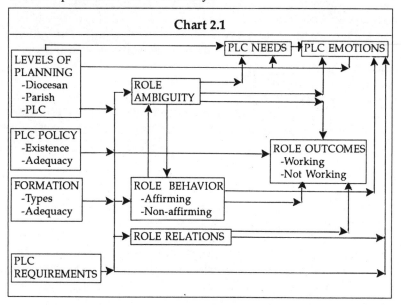

Chart 2.1

B. Demographic Profile

The sketch that follows, and the more detailed analysis of the role of policy, formation, requirements and planning upon PLC behavior and psychological state, are based on the information from the 102 PLCs who returned questionnaires in a form that could be used for analysis.

Religious status—PLCs overwhelmingly are women religious. Fully 79 percent of the respondents said that they were from a religious community and 75 percent described their status as sisters. The rest were married women (9 percent), permanent deacons (6 percent), married men (5 percent), single women (3 percent) and religious brothers (1 percent). No single lay men were found among the PLC sample.

Sex—As a large proportion of the sample are sisters or married and single women, the PLCs are predominantly female—86 percent vs. 14 percent male.

Therefore, when all data and analysis are presented below, it must be remembered that nearly 9 out of 10 of those doing parish life coordination today are female and 3 out of 4 are sisters. Why this type of work has drawn so many women and sisters can be explained by a variety of reasons. As a result of Vatican II and the subsequent changes in women's religious communities, many sisters and their communities began to seek work in settings that were new for them. The growth of the women's movement and the open discussion of women and the priesthood led some communities and some of their members to look to pastoral ministries in parishes. Coupled with this was the decline in the number of priests and the growth in the number of Catholic parishes. There was a clear need for more pastoral staff for these parishes and a concomitant push by women religious to enter pastoral ministries of various sorts.

This does not, however, explain why more lay women than lay men are found in PLC work (12 percent vs. 5 percent). The growth in interest in ministries of all sorts seems to have more of an impact on women than on men.

It is often said—and data would support—that men tend to avoid occupations in which women predominate. This would explain in part the reluctance of men to step into the role of pastoring a parish—even if that role traditionally has been occupied by other men. Problems inherent in the permanent diaconate may explain why only 6 percent of the sample are deacons. A bit of a mystery is why no single, non-ordained, lay men are found doing PLC work.

Marital status—Obviously, in light of the above demographics, 80 percent of PLCs have never married. Another 18 percent are presently married, 1 percent are divorced and now remarried, and 1 percent are widowed. Basically, therefore, we have the always-single or the always-married doing this form of ministry. It is interesting to note that just as traditional priest-pastors have been 100 percent single, the newer "pastors" are also overwhelmingly single. Still, those who hope to see more married persons in Church leadership can take heart that nearly 2 of 10 PLCs are married.

Years married—Among the married PLCs, 18 percent have been married for 10 years or less, 12 percent for 11-20 years, and 71 percent have been married for 21 or more years. Thus, the typical married PLC has been married for a number of years. This likely is explained by their more advanced age.

Number of Children—Again, as the data suggest, the majority (81 percent) of the PLCs have had no children. Among the married PLCs 8 percent have had one or two children, 6 percent have had three or four children, and 5 percent have had five or more children.

Age—The PLCs are a fairly homogeneous group when it comes to age. Only 6 percent are 40 years of age and under, 37 percent are from 40 to 50, 43 percent are 50 to 60, and 15 percent are over 60. So we must remember that 8 out of 10 PLCs are in the 40 to 60 category. This should come as no surprise

Table 2.1
Number of Parishes Served by the PLC

Size of Parish	Parish 1		Parish 2		Parish 3	
1-100 families	22	%	37	%	72	%
101-200	22		41		29	
201-300	19		9		-	
301-400	11		9		-	
401-500	6		-		-	
500+	19		5		-	

when one considers the skills, talents, knowledge and experience necessary to "pastor" a parish in the capacity of a PLC. Most persons in leadership capacities in any organization would be found within this same age span.

Education—In this category, as with age, PLCs are a homogeneous group. Fully 71 percent of the sample said that they had master's level degrees or beyond, 89 percent have a college degree or beyond, only 11 percent have some college, high school, technical school, or grade school education. Therefore, as a whole, PLCs are a highly educated group.

Type of education—We asked PLCs what kind of school they attended at each of the various levels of education. Nearly 75 percent of the sample had attended Catholic schools at the elementary, secondary or college levels.

Parish setting—PLCs were asked in which of four settings they did their work: the multiparish team, the parish cluster, one parish only, or several parishes. The most common setting is one parish (69 percent). The next most common setting is several parishes (20 percent). Therefore, nearly 9 of 10 PLCs work in one parish or two. Only 14 percent said that they served in a parish cluster in which separate parishes were yoked for some common activities such as religious education. Only 3 percent said that they worked with a multiparish team where several people shared the "pastoring" of several parishes. Clearly PLCs by and large are not working in teams and clusters, although nearly 2 of 10 do work in this setting.

Of the nearly 20 percent of PLCs who have more than one parish, the first parish is by far the largest parish in size and each of the other parishes is considerably smaller. The following table pinpoints this fact.

Parish locale—The PLCs were asked for the type of area in which their parish was located: 50 percent said rural or farm, 18 percent said town, 16 percent said their parish was in a resort area or urban fringe. Thus, fully 84 percent are serving parishes in rural and small town locales. Only 8 percent checked that their parish was in an urban or suburban location. Our sample of PLCs are serving in parishes that are more than 80 percent rural and small town.

Summary—We know from these demographic data that the typical PLC is as follows:

Table 2.2
Profile of Typical PLC

Single
Middle-aged
Female
A religious sister
Educated in Catholic schools
Advanced educated
Serving one parish not in a cluster or team setting
Serving in a rural or small town area

C. The Existence and Adequacy of a PLC Policy

In this section we will review the findings concerning the impact of PLC policies in the parish and diocese as such policies correlate with or affect role relations, psychological state, role ambiguity and role outcome among PLCs.

PLCs were asked about PLC policies in their diocese and parish. In general we wanted to know if contract stipulations existed, what lines of accountability were present in the diocese and parish, whether there was a diocesan plan for PLCs for the future, how the diocesan PLC plan was coordinated with the parish, and statements on how PLC work relates to the various ministries of the diocese and the parish. PLCs first were asked if such policies existed and, if they did, whether they considered the policies adequate or inadequate. Table 2.3 presents the averages for the entire group of PLC's on these two dimensions.

Based on both policy absence and inadequacy, PLCs would rank the following as the policies most needed by dioceses and parishes.

(1) Internship
(2) Coordination of parish and diocesan plans
(3) Relation with other diocesan ministries
(4) Diocesan plan
(5) Relation with other parish ministries

We now examine how these policy findings correlate with the four PLC conditions (variables) outlined at the beginning of this chapter.

Table 2.3
Rank in Terms of Adequacy

Area of Policy	Presence	Adequacy	Rank on Adequacy
Internship	1.82	2.83	3
Coordination of parish and diocesan plans	1.79	2.88	2
Relation with other diocesan ministries	1.74	2.74	4
Diocesan plan	1.73	3.07	1
Relation with other parish ministries	1.62	2.37	5
PLC contract	1.56	2.17	6
Parish accountability	1.56	2.13	8
Diocesan accountability	1.55	2.14	7
Length of contract specified	1.55	2.07	10
Full-time salary	1.40	2.09	9
Benefits provided	1.37	1.88	11

Presence: 1 = present; 2 = absent
Adequacy: 1 = very adequate; 2 = adequate; 3 = inadequate; 4 = very inadequate

1. Role Ambiguity

It could be argued that if the PLC believes policies are absent (either in the diocese or the parish) this could lead to role ambiguity. We will not attempt here to sketch out the inherent theological dimensions of role ambiguity, but rather concentrate on its sociological meaning. The term "role" has long been a workhorse of sociological explanation, role being defined as the sum total of all the expectations placed upon a person while in a given position. If we assume that the position upon which we are focusing is the "pastoring" of a parish in the absence of a resident priest (the PLC role), then, as with all other niches within the social structure of a group or an organization, certain expectations arise which govern the thought, feeling, behavior and relationships of persons performing that position.

The two most likely sources of constraint in the form of expectations for PLCs would be their diocese and their parish. We were concerned specifically with finding out if these expectations were ambiguous, i.e., lacking explicitness and clarity. Expectations also are internalized and form the conceptions the PLC has of her job. To some degree what is expected of the PLC is what she comes to expect of herself based on these internalized expectations from the diocese and the parish. Finally, how a PLC behaves is to some degree dependent upon these external diocesan and parish expectations and the expectations that get internalized.

So we conceptualized and measured role ambiguity in four different but related senses within both diocesan and parish expectations: (1) Are the expectations explicit? (2) Are the expectations clear? (3) Does the PLCs conception of her role agree with these expectations? (4) Is the PLCs performance consistent with the expectations? These four measures of role ambiguity are discussed in more detail later in the chapter and are summarized in Table 2.4 below, which incorporates role ambiguity averages for all PLCs.

These averages indicate that in general there is more ambiguity experienced by the PLC coming from parish than diocesan sources. Also, more ambiguity exists in terms of role expectations not being explicit and clear than from the conception the PLC has of her role agreeing with the diocese or parish, or the way she performs her role agreeing with the diocese and parish. So moderate amounts of ambiguity exist when measured in these sociologically defined ways.

We then correlated the various policies with the amount of ambiguity to test the notion that there would be more ambi-

Table 2.4
Measures of Role Ambiguity

Role Expectations	From Diocese	From Parish	
Are explicit	1.68	1.82	+
Are clear	1.61	1.75	+
Match PLC role conceptions	1.60	1.60	
Match PLC role performance	1.41	1.50	+

1 = Little ambiguity
2 = Some ambiguity
+ = More ambiguity

guity for the PLC when she considered PLC policies (which can be seen as expectations) absent or inadequate.

Role ambiguity from absence of diocesan policy—On all four indicators of role ambiguity (clarity, explicitness, conception and performance) there is a relationship with the absence of policies: when the PLC perceives that these policies do not exist she feels more role ambiguity coming from the diocese as measured in the four ways. In particular, the policies that contribute the most to this sense of ambiguity are found below.

Role ambiguity from inadequacy of diocesan policy— Whether the PLCs find these various policies adequate or not

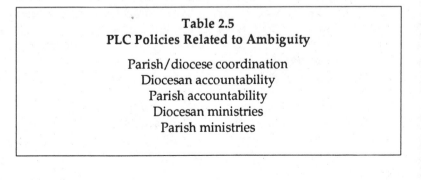

Table 2.5
PLC Policies Related to Ambiguity

Parish/diocese coordination
Diocesan accountability
Parish accountability
Diocesan ministries
Parish ministries

does not seem to be quite as important as their mere existence. However, on at least the clear and explicit indicators of role ambiguity, the relationship is such that the more inadequate the PLC judges these policies, the more role ambiguity she is experiencing. In particular, the following policies that are judged to be inadequate seem to contribute most to the PLCs ambiguity about her job.

Table 2.6
Diocesan Policies and Role Ambiguity

Diocesan ministries
Parish ministries
Salary policy
Contract policy
Diocesan accountability
Benefits
Internship

So in general, having policies and having adequate policies plays a role in the overall clarity with which the PLC operates. No policies or inadequate policies means she feels ambiguous about her role with reference to diocesan expectations. The PLCs seem to be saying that to have no policy is worse than to have policies that are inadequate. Policies in existence can always be changed and modified. Policies have a way of shaking out dialogue and education. No policy means the PLC is left on her own. Perhaps part of the problem in this area comes from the fact that the role of PLC is not defined by a theology of ordination so much as a theology of Church. Perhaps dioceses spend more planning time in discussing the identity of the priesthood rather than the identity of the PLC. This could account for much of the ambiguity that we have found exists in the PLC role.

Role ambiguity from presence of parish policy—A reverse pattern tends to emerge when we look at role ambiguity from parish sources. The more policies are perceived to be present, the more ambiguity the PLC feels. In particular, when there are (a) benefits and (b) a diocesan PLC plan, role ambiguity is higher. However, when parish ministries and diocesan ministries policies are absent there is more role ambiguity. A more mixed pattern was found.

Role ambiguity from inadequacy of parish policy—In general, the more inadequate the PLC finds these policies, the more ambiguity see feels coming from the parish. In particular, where parish ministries, contract length and an internship policy are inadequate, higher levels of role ambiguity coming from parish sources are found. One exception to this pattern is that when PLCs find a diocesan PLC plan to be adequate they express higher levels of role ambiguity from parish sources.

Table 2.7
Inadequate Policies and Parish Ambiguity

Parish ministries
Contract length
Internship

While a totally consistent pattern was not found, in general when policies are absent or inadequate, higher levels of ambiguity were expressed. The one major deviation from this, as we have seen, is that PLCs express higher levels of role ambiguity from parish sources when certain of these policies are present. One gets the feeling that policies often cause the PLC to be caught between the parish and the diocese. To follow the diocesan guidelines may lead to difficulties with the parish.

Part of the problem the PLC must deal with is that parishioners have many of the same pastoral expectations of a PLC as they would of a pastor. From the parishioner's perspective, the question is why the PLC can't do more to meet parishioner needs. The PLC, on the other hand, is operating under directives from the bishop and feels some limitations to her role with respect to the parishioner. Thus the PLC is often caught in the middle. When she agrees and follows the often conservative guidelines coming from her bishop and the diocese, she may not be fulfilling the needs of her parishioners, needs which may be greater than the way in which the diocese has defined her jurisdiction. While parishioners may not know what the diocesan policy is, they know when the PLC is not meeting their needs. Thus the PLC pleases the diocese but displeases the parish.

It is also likely that a number of unspoken expectations are placed on the PLC as a woman doing something very unconventional in the parish. There may exist a subtle shift in expectations as a woman takes over the work of the man who was their pastor. These expectations may have more to do with conflicting expectations between men and women than between pastor and parishioners.

Some parishioners may engage in a type of passive-aggressive behavior toward both the diocese and the PLC. They may not speak up, and simply become passively aggressive toward the PLC. On the other hand, they may feel more free to speak up to the PLC than they did to a priest-pastor. The PLC may get the brunt of parishioner hostility toward the diocese as displaced hostility.

Table 2.8 Emotional State of the PLC		
Emotional State	*Average*	
Frustrated	1.81	(Most negative)
Exhausted	1.73	
Unsupported by priests	1.59	
Inadequately prepared	1.52	
Unaccomplished	1.48	
Not like a pastor	1.43	
Unsupported by bishop	1.41	
Full of vision	1.40	
Not burned out	1.40	
Successful	1.39	
Hopeful	1.32	
Not like dropping out	1.25	
Needed	1.23	
Like an insider	1.17	
Well received	1.16	(Most positive)

2. The Emotional State of the PLC

The PLCs were asked how they felt about their PLC role in their parish. They were given a list of 16 emotional states and asked at what level they identified with these states. The following is a rank ordering of 15 of these emotional states. In general, the PLCs were having the most negative emotions in the areas of being frustrated, exhausted, being unsupported and inadequately prepared. On the other hand, PLC's were experiencing the most positive emotions in the form of being well received, feeling like an insider, being needed and hopeful.

Emotions and the presence of PLC policies—It would seem that the presence of various PLC policies creates both positive and negative moods in PLCs, as the list below indicates:

Table 2.9	
Emotions and the Prescence/Absense of PLC Policies	
Emotions when Policies Present	*Emotions when Policies Absent*
Like an outsider	Not supported by bishop
Not needed	Lacking in vision
Burned out	Not hopeful
Exhausted	Not supported by priests
	Like dropping out
	Unsuccessful

The table may indicate that the PLC feels burnt out and exhausted under the presence of too many PLC policies. It is possible that being a woman doing a man's job in a largely male diocesan atmosphere may make one feel like an outsider or not needed even when the diocese does provide a well-spelled-out PLC policy. In particular, *specific* policies seem to be related to specific emotions. The most common emotional response to these policies is "feeling like dropping out." The following table is a summary of this:

Table 2.10
Emotional State Relative to Type of Policy

Type of Policy	Emotional State
Diocesan plan absent	Lacking vision
Coordinated policy absent	Like dropping out
	Unaccomplished
	Not well received
Diocesan accountability absent	Unsuccessful
	Unsupported by bishop
Parish accountability absent	Not hopeful
	Not full of vision
Contract length absent	Like dropping out
Internship present	Like dropping out
Diocesan plan present	Burned out
	Exhausted

Emotions and adequacy of PLC policies—When the adequacy of policies were considered the pattern emerged as found in Table 2.12.

In particular, the following policies were related to specific emotions. The most common emotional response to these

Table 2.11
Emotions and the Adequacy of Policies

Emotions when Policies Adequate	Emotions when Policies Inadequate
Frustrated	Like an outsider
Not well received	Not needed
Not hopeful	Unsuccessful
Not supported by bishop	
Not supported by priests	
Not pastoral	
Unaccomplished	
Without vision	

Table 2.12
Policies Related to Specific Emotions

Policies	Specific Emotions
Diocesan accountability inadequate	Unsupported by bishop
	Unsupported by priests
	Not pastoral
Salary policy adequate	Not full of vision
Contract policy adequate	Not pastoral
Benefits policy inadequate	Frustrated
	Hopeless
	Unsupported by bishop
	Not pastoral
	Inadequately prepared
	Burned out
Salary policy inadequate	Frustrated
	Exhausted

policies was "feeling unsupported by the bishop," "burned out" and "not pastoral."

3. PLC Policy and Affirming Relations

PLCs were asked to describe relations with their canonical pastor and their sacramental ministers that were of an affirming nature (behaviors that build a person up). Based upon Monette, PLCs were given ten situations in which the canonical pastor and sacramental minister could affirm the relationship between themselves and the PLC. The situations were (1) invites PLC to take a visible leadership role at the liturgy, (2) channels to PLC requests of parishioners, e.g. for baptisms and other decisions, (3) repeatedly instructs the parish about the new leadership structure in the parish, (4) regularly monitors his relationship with PLC for possible role confusion, (5) defers to PLC's judgment on sacramental matters, (6) trusts PLC in "pastoring" role, (7) shows flexibility toward PLC's joint ministry to the parish, (8) demonstrates resourcefulness and skill in this new form of ministry, (9) submits problems in joint ministry to prayer, and (10) encourages PLC to preach. The following table ranks these ten situations in terms of the

PLC's responses, from the least affirming behavior at the top to the most affirming at the bottom.

The first generalization that can be made based upon these data is that according to PLC perceptions, canonical pastors show less affirming behaviors than do sacramental ministers. In nearly all of the ten settings presented above, the scores (averages) are higher (more negative) for the canonical pastors than for the sacramental ministers. In two areas, however, regularly monitoring his relationship with PLC for possible role confusion and inviting the PLC to take a visible leadership role at the liturgy, canonical pastors show more positive, affirming behavior toward the PLC. In these two areas, the sacramental ministers get their highest negative scores, indicating problem areas in the relationship. In other words, sacramental ministers have the most difficulty when it comes to monitoring the PLC-sacramental minister relationship for confusion and in showing the PLC how to take a visible leadership role at the liturgy.

Both of these seem to be because of the more intimate relationship that exists between the person celebrating the Mass

Table 2.13 Policy and Affirming Relations		
Affirming Relations	*Canonical Pastor*	*Sacramental Minister*
Confusion	3.12+	3.18- Least affirming
Preach	2.93-	2.88+
Leadership	2.89+	3.46-
Prayer	2.82-	2.63+
Sacramental judgment	2.52-	1.90+
Liturgy	2.47	-----
Resourcefulness	2.26-	2.08+
Joint ministry	1.90-	1.71+
Pastoring	1.51-	1.43+ Most affirming
+ = More positive - = More negative 1 = Very often; 2 = Often; 3 = Sometimes; 4 = Seldom		

and sacraments (the sacramental minister) and the PLC. The canonical pastor would normally take a more hands-off approach and give guidance from a distance and less frequently. It cannot be known for sure from these data whether the relationship between canonical pastors and PLCs are truly more negative or whether, because of the nature of a canonical pastor, fewer opportunities for affirming behaviors exist. It is, perhaps, comforting to know that for the more usual day-in, day-out relations, PLCs and sacramental ministers have the more affirmed relationship.

Policy absence and affirming relations with the canonical pastor—We tested the idea that the more PLC policies were absent the less affirming would be the relations between the PLC and the canonical pastor. For the 11 policies we studied, the data in general do support the idea that if policies are absent, a less affirming relation will exist with the canonical pastor. In particular the following policies were most related to nonaffirming relations:

Table 2.14 Policy Absence and Affirming Relation	
Type of Policy Absent	*Type of Affirming Behavior Absemt with Canonical Pastor*
Diocesan ministries	Sacramental judgment
Diocesan plan	Resourcefulness Preach
Coordinated policy	Sacramental judgment Prayerfulness
Diocesan accountability	Prayerfulness Resourcefulness

It would appear from these data that when there is no plan that shows how the PLC ministry fits into the ministries of the diocese, no plan to coordinate a PLC plan with the parish and no accountability to the diocese, the canonical pastor will have more difficulty demonstrating resourcefulness and skill in this new form of ministry, deferring sacramental matters to the PLC's judgment, submitting problems in the joint ministry to prayer and encouraging the PLC to preach.

Policy inadequacy and affirming relations with the canonical pastor—When policies are looked at in terms of their adequacy and not their mere existence some of the same policies emerge as important, but this time an additional set materializes.

Two sets of conclusions can be reached when we look at how PLCs feel about the adequacy of PLC policy and its connection to affirming behavior. Based on the above table, the inadequacies found in one set of policies (diocesan ministries, coordinated policy and diocesan accountability) lead to the following difficulties in the PLC-canonical pastor relation: the canonical pastor does not defer judgment on sacramental matters to the PLC and does not submit problems in the joint ministry to prayerfulness. A second set of policies judged to be inadequate (contract, its benefits, contract length and the opportunity for an internship) presage the following difficulties in the PLC-canonical pastor relation: lack of monitoring

---

Table 2.15
Policy Inadequacy and Affirming Relations

Type of Inadequate Policy	*Type of Affirming Behavior Absent with Canonical Pastor*
Policy Set I	
Diocesan ministries	Sacramental judgment Prayerfulness
Coordinated policy	Sacramental judgment
Diocesan accountability	Sacramental judgment Pastoring
Policy Set II	
Contract	Confusion monitoring
Benefits	Pastoring Joint ministry
Contract length	Pastoring
Internship	Confusion monitoring

for possible role confusion, not trusting the PLC in a "pastoring" role and not showing flexibility toward the joint ministry.

Table 2.16
Inadequate PLC Policies and
PLC/Canonical Pastor Relations
Contract
Benefits
Contract length
Internship

So our data have shown that, in the judgment of the PLC at least, when dioceses do not have policies in the areas of diocesan ministries, PLC plans, coordinated PLC plans with parishes and accountability, canonical pastors develop negative relations with their PLCs in the areas of sacramental judgment, prayerfulness, resourcefulness and preaching.

Table 2.17
Policy Absence and Negative
PLC/Canonical Pastor Relations
Sacramental judgment
Prayerfulness
Resourcefulness
Preaching

Likewise, if they do not have adequate policies dealing with PLC contracts, benefits, contract length and internships for PLCs, they run the risk of negative relations between the canonical pastor and the PLC in terms of confusion over roles, lack of trust in the PLC in her "pastoring" role and not showing flexibility toward the joint ministry in the parish.

Policy absence and inadequacy and affirming relations with the sacramental minister—The number of PLCs who said that policies were either absent or inadequate and admitted to negative affirming behaviors was too small for us to make any valid generalizations, and we will attempt no summaries. We will try to draw more succinct conclusions on the connections between PLC policy and affirming relations in the concluding chapter.

Table 2.18
Policy Inadequacy and Poor
PLC/Canonical Pastor Relations

Role confusion
Lack of trust in "pastoring" role
Lack of flexibility in joint ministry

---

4. PLC Policy and Nonaffirming Relations

The PLCs were presented with a list of six nonaffirming (tearing down) situations and asked how often their canonical pastor and sacramental minister engaged in each of them. The specific situations were: (1) How often do you have uncomfortable feelings like hurt, anger and fear? (2) How often do you have disagreements or confrontations? (3) How often do you have crises in collaboration in "pastoring"? (4) How often are you treated in an unequal or discriminatory fashion? (5) How often are you treated as an incompetent? and (6) How often do you have poor gender dynamics? The table below presents the rank ordering of each of these for both the canonical pastor and the sacramental minister. The averages for all of the PLCs who responded are presented.

Table 2.19		
Nonaffirming Relations	*Canonical Pastor*	*Sacramental Minister*
Uncomfortable feelings	3.98-	4.09+
Disagreements/ confrontations	4.11+	4.02-
Collaboration crises	4.25-	4.35+
Poor gender dynamics	4.25-	4.39+
Treated unequally	4.27+	4.25-
Treated as incompetent	4.70+	4.64-
3 = Sometimes	+= More positive	
4 = Seldom	- = More negative	
5 = Never		

Inspection of the table shows that in the whole of the six indicators no more negative relations exist with the canonical pastor than with the sacramental minister, although in three indicators individually there are more negative relations with the canonical pastor, and three others show more positive relations with the canonical pastors. It may be significant, however, that the canonical pastors have more negative relations with their PLCs in terms of uncomfortable feelings, crises in collaboration and poor gender dynamics. It should be pointed out, however, that PLCs overall do not describe their relations with either their canonical pastors or their sacramental ministers as negative. On the average, they say they seldom or never have such kinds of nonaffirming experiences with these priests with whom they work.

Policy absence and nonaffirming relations with the canonical pastor—We sought to test the idea that the more PLC policies were absent, the more negative the nonaffirming relations would be. The data did confirm this notion, even though the number of PLCs who admitted to negative relations with their canonical pastor and who felt policies were absent was small. Certain specific types of policies likewise were related to specific nonaffirming types of relations. These are summarized below.

It can be seen from this table that the lack of certain PLC policies results primarily in three kinds of nonaffirming behaviors being displayed by the canonical pastors: (1) collaboration crises in "pastoring" the parish, (2) disagreements and confrontations and (3) treating the PLC in an unequal, discriminatory fashion. The policies that are believed to be absent and leading to these behaviors principally concern diocesan and parish planning and contract issues.

Policy inadequacy and nonaffirming relations with the canonical pastor—The number of PLCs who admitted to nonaffirming relations with their canonical pastors and who also talked about policies being inadequate was even smaller than those in the policy absence data reported above. Therefore, drawing valid generalizations is hazardous at best. Nonetheless, the same pattern emerged in which the more the PLC admits certain policies are inadequate, the more she says she has had various kinds of nonaffirming experiences with her canonical

Table 2.20
Policy Absence and Nonaffirming Relations
with the Canonical Pastor

Type of Policy Absent	*Type of Nonaffirming Relations*
Diocesan ministries	Disagreements
	Collaboration crises
	Poor gender dynamics
Parish ministries	Disagreements
	Collaboration crises
	Made to feel incompetent
Coordinated policy	Disagreements
	Collaboration crises
Diocesan accountability	Disagreements
	Collaboration crises
	Inequality
Parish accountability	Collaboration crises
	Inequality
Salary	Collaboration crises
Contract Length	Collaboration crises
	Inequality
Internship	Uncomfortable
	Collaboration crises
	Inequality

pastor. When we checked the data for relations between specific kinds of policies and specific nonaffirming behavior, the pattern found below resulted.

As we look at the data, keeping in mind the inadequacy of PLC policies as based on PLC perceptions, a general pattern emerges in which inadequate policies and nonaffirming relations are found together. Specifically, inadequate policies concerning diocesan and parish ministries, diocesan accountability, salary and benefits lead to a wide array of negative, nonaffirming behaviors. Five of the six nonaffirming behaviors presented to the PLCs for evaluation are found to be related to inadequate policies. While three of these six policies were related to nonaffirming behavior when we checked for

Table 2.21	
Policy Inadequacy and Nonaffirming Relations	
with the Canonical Pastor	

Type of Inadequate Policy	*Type of Nonaffirming Relations*
Diocesan ministries	Disagreements
	Collaborations crises
	Made to feel incompetent
	Poor gender dynamics
Parish ministries	Disagreements
	Collaboration crises
	Made to feel incompetent
	Poor gender dynamics
Diocesan Accountability	Uncomfortable
Salary Policy	Uncomfortable
	Collaboration crises
	Made to feel incompetent
	Poor gender dynamics
Benefits	Uncomfortable
	Disagreements
	Collaboration crises
	Made to feel incompetent

absent policies, fully five of the six were present when we looked at the inadequacy of the same policies.

Policy absence or inadequacy and the sacramental minister— As only a small number of PLCs reported that their sacramental ministers treated them in nonaffirming ways when various policies were either absent or inadequate, no generalizations will be attempted.

Relations between the PLC and the canonical pastor or the sacramental minister do not appear to present a clear-cut situation. When we asked the PLCs to describe candidly their relationship with both the canonical pastor and the sacramental minister, the PLCs told us that in general they relate more poorly to the sacramental minister and, therefore, relate more positively to the canonical pastor. However, when these two positions were compared on the 9 different areas of affirming relations we presented to PLCs, the sacramental minister emerged with more positive relations in 6 of 8 of areas. This means that the canonical pastor relationship was rated higher in only 2 of the 8 affirming relations. This would seem to contradict the PLCs' contention that relations with the sacramental minister are more strained than with the canonical pastor. Moreover, when we look at the quantity of nonaffirming relations between the PLC and the canonical pastor or the sacramental minister, no pattern emerges—canonical pastors are given higher ratings on as many of the nonaffirming behaviors as are the sacramental ministers.

Thus, from the data available to us, all we can conclude is that in general PLCs say they have poorer relations with their sacramental ministers, whereas they say their sacramental ministers demonstrate more affirming relations toward them than do their canonical pastors.

Some observations may clarify these findings. PLCs and canonical pastors are more likely to conflict over policy, whereas PLCs and sacramental ministers are more likely to conflict over procedures. Also, canonical pastors may visit the parish only several times a year or have little part in the day-to-day activities of the parish. Therefore, disagreements have less chance to develop with the canonical pastor than with the sacramental minister, who is present more often.

D. PLCs and Role Ambiguity

1. Causes of Role Ambiguity

The sociological literature has pointed out for some time that roles are the major way in which social life becomes organized. Roles are the culturally prescribed ways that we are to act, think, feel and relate in a given social position. For various social, political, economic and religious reasons, many roles emerge only over time, while others disintegrate. In both cases there is lacking a specific set of expectations as to how persons in these undefined roles should act, think, feel and relate. Social scientists label this lack of expectations as role ambiguity.

Role ambiguity therefore is attributable to four conditions: (1) societies lacking a clear idea of what should be expected and therefore not making expectations clear to their members, (2) societies lacking explicit guidelines, norms, laws, rules or operating procedures to convey their expectations of their members, (3) individual members having conceptions— ideas, values, motivations, knowledge—from their own social- ization, or formation, that do not match those of their socie- ties, and (4) the performance of the individual not matching the expectations of these societies. The more of these condi- tions that exist, the more a given role is ambiguous.

Moreover, research has demonstrated that there are cer- tain consequences of role ambiguity. For the individual, a number of largely negative emotional, motivational and need states emerge. For the society, members' behavior becomes unreliable, and interpersonal relations lack harmony and reci- procity.

Within the context of our larger study of PLCs, we wanted to test some of these ideas concerning role ambiguity in the role of the parish life coordinator. It could be argued that the PLC role already is both theologically and sociologi- cally ambiguous. The Catholic church in the U.S. has wit- nessed an ever increasing movement toward lay ministry and lay involvement in religious affairs. As noted in the Introduc- tion, the shortage of priests and the reawakening of the proper understanding of the duties and rights of Baptism enkindled by the Second Vatican Council have created a climate in which the Church is reexamining the proper role of the laity vis-a-vis the clergy.

The 1983 revision of Canon Law proposed a new role, but then left vague the exact structural manifestations such a new role would take. The Code argued that lay persons could be used to "administer" (if not "pastor") a parish when no resi- dent priest was available, as long as this person was under the pastoral supervision of a priest. In a day-to-day sense, how- ever, it quickly becomes unclear as to how far this role enters into pastoral oversight and supervision. Expectations from the larger Church, the dioceses and the parishes in which PLCs are placed were unclear and their guidelines and operating procedures not very explicit. Furthermore the conceptions that PLCs held in their own minds of the PLC role were a product of varying formal and informal formation. The conceptions of the PLCs could vary widely from the conceptions of both the parish and diocese. Finally, how a given PLC performed her role could itself deviate from diocesan or parish expectations. The Church had done a thorough job of socializing this particular generation of adult Catholics as to proper behavior for both laity and priests. Many Catholics were sure they knew what Father was supposed to do and what they were supposed to do. Now, however, all this is much more *ambiguous*.

To bring to this question of role ambiguity some clarity from social science, we tested the following model, grounding it in the data that we have collected from parish life coordinators.

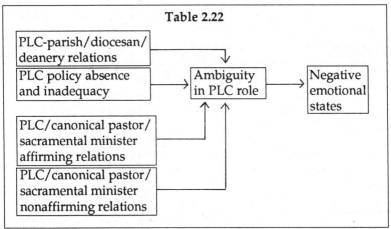

Table 2.22

Earlier, in Section C, The Existence and Adequacy of a PLC Policy," we measured role ambiguity in the four ways proposed. We also asked the PLCs to answer in an additional two ways: (1) as they perceived these expectations coming from their diocese and (2) as they perceived these expectations coming from their parish. Altogether we had eight measures of role ambiguity, as summarized in Table 2.4. As this point, we present evidence to confirm the model of role ambiguity we outlined immediately above, beginning with role ambiguity coming from diocesan sources.

We argue that when PLC policies are insufficiently institutionalized this condition will create an environment in which strained relations will exist between the PLC, the canonical pastor, the sacramental minister, the parish, deanery and the diocese. These strained relations will lead to high role ambiguity which itself will result in negative emotional states in the PLC.

2. Diocesan Sources of Role Ambiguity

Role ambiguity and nonaffirming relations—Our data reveals a general pattern. Where nonaffirming relations with the sacramental minister and the canonical pastor are of a negative variety, role ambiguity from the diocese is higher. This means that where relations between the priests and the PLC involve negative feelings, disagreements, crises in collaboration, feelings of inequality and negative gender dynamics, higher levels of ambiguity from diocesan sources are present. Of the four conditions creating role ambiguity described above, the greatest significance for the PLC involves the first condition, *when dioceses do not make clear what they expect of the PLC.* When this happens she experiences a wide range of nonaffirming relations with both the canonical pastor and the sacramental minister. As we have seen, expectations define roles--and roles define relationships. When these expectations are either not clear, explicit or when the conception and behavior of the PLC differs from these expectations, the PLC feels role ambiguity.

It is possible to think of this in reverse also, i.e., because there is role ambiguity, the relations between PLC and priests are nonaffirming. It is likely that the factors mutually affect each other. Poor relations lead to ambiguity, and ambiguity leads to increasingly poor relations.

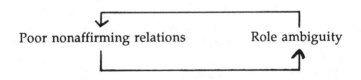

Poor nonaffirming relations   Role ambiguity

Role ambiguity and affirming relations—When we tested the connection between the affirming relations and role ambiguity, the same pattern emerged. When these affirming relations between both the canonical pastor and the sacramental minister and the PLC were negative, higher levels of role ambiguity emerged. Specifically this means that when PLCs are experiencing problems in their relations (in the areas outlined above, such as taking a visible leadership role at the liturgy, channeling to the PLC requests from the parishioners, etc.) they also admit to higher degrees of ambiguity in their PLC role. Again, if dioceses are not making clear and explicit their expectations to their PLCs or the conceptions and performance of the PLC does not match with what the diocese wants, we would expect some difficulties in the relation between the PLC and her canonical pastor and/or sacramental minister. If expectations are unclear, then it is likely that any one of the above problems would materialize.

It is also likely that role ambiguity and nonaffirming relations are reciprocally related and reinforce each other in the following fashion:

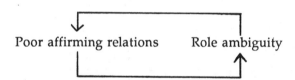

Poor affirming relations   Role ambiguity

Role ambiguity and PLCs' relationship with others in diocese, parish, deanery—PLCs were asked to describe the quality of their relations with (1) the parish, (2) the priests and deanery and (3) the diocese. They were asked how these relationships were at the time they first came to the parish and how they are now. The following table gives the ranks based on the average responses of the PLCs to these questions.

Several generalizations can be made about PLC relations based on the above two tables. (1) Relations when the PLC first came to the parish could be described as good to adequate, (2) relations in the present show considerable improvement, described as good to excellent, (3) when PLCs first came to their parishes they experienced the most negative relations with those close to them in the parish or deanery, and the most positive relations with diocesan officials and the bishop, (4) in relationships now, this has reversed—with the most negative relations being with the deanery, diocesan officials and the bishop and the most positive being with the parish, (5) the

Table 2.23

Relation	Now	When First Came to Parish
Deanery	*1.86+	*2.19
Diocesan officials	1.71+	1.88
Bishop	1.69 -	1.67
Sacramental minister	1.57+	2.03
Canonical pastor	1.51+	1.91
Parish staff	1.44+	2.08
Parishioners	1.43+	2.40
Parish council	1.42+	2.20

* These scores are averages for all PLC's.

1 = Excellent + means an improved relation from when PLC first came to the parish

2 = Good

3 = Adequate

Table 2.24

Relation	When First Came to Parish	Now
Parishioners	*2.40	*1.43+
Parish council	2.20	1.42+
Deanery	2.19	1.86+
Parish staff	2.08	1.44+
Sacramental minister	2.03	1.57+
Canonical pastor	1.91	1.51+
Diocesan officials	1.88	1.71+
Bishop	1.67	1.69-

* Scores are averages for all PLCs.

1 = Excellenent+ means improved relations since moving to the parish

2 = Good

3 = Adequate

PLCs have had a dramatic improvement in relations with their parishes, (6) there has been only a small improvement in relations with diocesan officials, and (7) while diocesan relations have slightly improved, relatively speaking they are the poorest of all of those in the present situation and (8) there has been a very slight deterioration with the bishop.

We speculated that, as with relations with the canonical pastor and the sacramental minister, negative relations with others in the parish, deanery and diocese would also predict higher amounts of role ambiguity. In general, this pattern was upheld by our data. When relations with parishioners, parish staff, parish council, the canonical pastor, the sacramental minister, the deanery priests, diocesan officials and the bishop are more negative, higher degrees of role ambiguity occur. Some conclusions based on these data are: (1) ambiguity and poor relations are stronger now than before, (2) ambiguity and poor relations are especially related to the canonical pastor, diocesan officials and the bishop, indicating that supraparish relations contribute more to ambiguity than the parish, (3) the strongest indicator of role ambiguity is the first indicator— negative relations materialize most often when expectations from the diocese are not clear.

PLC policy and role ambiguity—Earlier in this chapter we presented evidence that, in general, when PLC policies are either absent or inadequate, higher levels of ambiguity were found. We noted one major deviation from this pattern. When certain policies are present, PLCs feel more ambiguity coming from their parishioners. We commented then that PLCs may feel that they are trapped between what their diocese wants and what their parishioners want, leading them to experience even greater amounts of role conflict. (Role conflict is different from role ambiguity. It rises not when expectations are unclear but when expectations contradict each other.)

Role ambiguity and the resulting emotional states of the PLC—Our model predicted that more negative emotional states would exist when role ambiguity was higher. Since PLCs would not know what was expected of them, or their conception and performance of the role would not match the expectations of their dioceses, it could be conjectured that the PLC might experience more exhaustion, lack of success, burnout, frustration, and the like. The data do indeed back upon this speculation. The full range of the 16 emotional states presented to the PLCs are associated with one or several of the indicators of role ambiguity. Role ambiguity seems most related to the following types of emotional response presented in rank order with the emotions most related to ambiguity at the top of the list.

Table 2.25
Emotions related to Role Ambiguity

1. Unsuccessful
2. Unneeded
3. Hopeless
4. Lacking in vision
5. Inadequately prepared
6. Burned out
7. Frustrated
8. Unaccomplished

The clarity indicator of role ambiguity did not predict these emotional states as well as the explicit, conception and performance indicators.

3. Parishioner Sources of Role Ambiguity

PLCs also were given the chance to say how much ambiguity in their role they thought came from the parish rather than the diocese. We have just reported that the diocese is indeed a source of ambiguity to PLCs. The data for parish ources of ambiguity, while consistent with this general pattern, nonetheless is not as strong.

Role ambiguity and nonaffirming relations with sacramental minister—There is a weak tendency in the data to support the pattern reported in the previous section on diocesan sources of ambiguity: that is, where nonaffirming relations are negative, more role ambiguity from the parish is expressed. The numbers of PLCs having negative nonaffirming relations and also expressing role ambiguity were too small for an adequate test of this relationship in the data. It will be presented simply as weak evidence in support of the original finding.

Role ambiguity and affirming relations with sacramental minister—While the numbers are sufficient to test this association, the data do not warrant making any general conclusion. The variables do not seem to be correlated.

Role ambiguity and nonaffirming relations with canonical pastor—While the number of PLCs answering these questions was higher, there is simply no clear pattern in the data.

Role ambiguity and affirming relations with canonical pastor—While the numbers are sufficient to test this relationship, the data show only a weak association such that we can say that negative affirming relations are somewhat associated with role ambiguity. None of these relations are statistically significant, however.

Our data allow us only minimal support of the contention that, when it comes to parishioner sources of role ambiguity, the more negative the relations the more the role ambiguity. We could not uphold this contention for nonaffirming relations with the sacramental minister and for affirming relations with the canonical pastor. In the two cases where the data lean in the direction of the hypothesis, the evidence is much less strong than in the case of role ambiguity coming from diocesan sources. So we reach the overall conclusion that the diocese presents itself as a stronger source of role ambiguity to the PLC than does the parish. This would seem to contradict the conclusion reached above under the section on policy and role ambiguity. There we argued that, in general, more ambiguity seems to come from parishioner sources. However, when we relate ambiguity to its possible sources (such as poor affirming and nonaffirming relations and relations in general), the diocese emerges as a potentially bigger source of ambiguity. Any contradiction is perhaps explained by the fact that we did not get as large a response from PLCs relating to parishioner sources of ambiguity. Therefore, we may have simply not been able to get a good test of this idea.

Role ambiguity and PLCs' relationships with others—We found with diocesan sources of ambiguity that the more negative the PLCs relations with the parish, deanery and diocese, the higher would be her role ambiguity. Our data on parishioner sources of ambiguity reveals the same pattern. On all types of relationships (whether in the parish, deanery or diocese) the more negative these relations, the higher the role ambiguity. We found this relationship to be stronger in the present situation than when the PLC first came to the parish.

Role ambiguity and the emotional states of the PLC—It would seem that it is as likely for the PLC to experience negative emotions coming from parishioner sources of role ambiguity as it would be from diocesan sources. Our data confirm this. PLCs who have higher states of parishioner-induced role ambiguity do experience a wide variety of negative emotional states such as feeling unsuccessful, exhausted, and the like. There is, however, no evidence that ambiguity and negative affects are any more strongly connected when the source of the ambiguity is the parish than when it is the diocese.

The best predictors of negative emotion are the conception and performance indicators of role ambiguity and the following are the emotions most strongly associated with role ambiguity.

Table 2.26
Emotions Most Connected with Ambiguity

Feeling unaccomplished

Feeling unsuccessful

Exhaustion

Not being received by the parish

Not pastoral

Not needed

Not hopeful

Lacking in vision

Unsupported by the bishop

Recapitulation—Our data give strong support to the model of role ambiguity introduced at the beginning of this section. We can feel confident in concluding that (1) negative relations with parish, deanery and diocese, (2) negative affirming and nonaffirming relations with the canonical pastor and perhaps the sacramental minister and (3) absent and inadequate PLC policies give rise to ambiguity both from diocesan and parish sources. We pointed out that it may also be that ambiguity in the PLC role is giving rise to these negative relations. Furthermore, higher levels of role ambiguity are related to negative emotional states in the PLC. These findings suggest that to improve the overall psychological well-being of the PLC, dioceses and parishes should construct and put into operation policies which are more adequate. This would lead to more positive relations between the PLC and those with whom she associates. Our data presented earlier show that absent or inadequate PLC policies are associated with negative affirming and nonaffirming behaviors and these poor relations in turn are associated with role ambiguity.

E. PLCs and Perceptions of Planning Adequacy

The PLCs in our study were asked to elaborate on the role ambiguities they mentioned by responding whether inadequacies in diocesan and parish planning as well as their own formation in becoming a PLC were responsible for their role ambiguities. These open-ended responses were coded into either adequate or inadequate planning categories and were formulated under three dimensions: diocesan planning, parish planning and PLC planning (their own formation). All three of these were follow-up questions to one asking the PLC if she admitted to having some role ambiguity. We then correlated these three evaluations of planning with the major variables guiding our study of PLCs. We tested the following notions: (1) that where the PLC said that planning was inadequate she would also say that PLC policy was either absent or inadequate, (2) that when the PLC thought planning was adequate she would also say that things were working out with her PLC role, (3) that when the PLC thought planning was inadequate she would also say that her role was ambiguous and (4) that when the PLC thought planning was inadequate she would admit to more negative emotional states. We present the evidence on each of these three types of planning.

1. Diocesan Planning

Absence and inadequacy of PLC planning—As hypothesized, when the PLC perceives that diocesan planning for PLC matters has been inadequate, she also believes that PLC policies are absent. Due to too small numbers in the sample who said that planning was inadequate and that PLC policies were inadequate, we could not test the notion that when planning is inadequate the PLC will contend that PLC policy has been inadequate. It is likely that the PLC makes a global evaluation of her diocese, in that if the diocese does not have policies dealing with parish life coordination then it must have poor planning. Those who answered this question also admitted that they had some role ambiguity coming from diocesan sources. This further piece of information seems to confirm the idea that PLCs are experiencing role conflict because they find their diocesan planning process for PLCs to be inadequate. Between one half and one third of the PLC sample felt that diocesan policies were absent, and of these more felt that diocesan planning was inadequate than felt was adequate.

Diocesan planning and what is working—The PLCs were asked an open-ended question concerning what they thought was working with the PLC model implemented in their parish. When their answers were tallied, the five most common responses are summarized below:

Table 2.26
What Is Working About the PLC Role in Your Parish?
Acceptance by parish
Enabling of parishioners
Service to people
Adequate authority to enact the PLC role
Good relations with parishioners

When PLCs said they thought that diocesan planning was adequate, they also tended to say that they felt things were working out in their PLC ministry. This is further evidence that when dioceses have carefully planned for pastoral administration work with their parishes and with the PLCs who will serve them, these PLCs have a greater sense that things are going well.

Diocesan planning and parish role ambiguity—We tested to see if there would be more role ambiguity from parishioner sources when PLCs said that diocesan planning was inadequate. One would presume that if things are not properly taken care of at the diocesan level, this could affect the PLCs' performance in the parish and also affect parishioners' perceptions of what is expected of the PLC. This idea was not confirmed by the data. Instead we found the opposite: when PLCs perceived that diocesan planning was adequate they experienced more role ambiguity from parishioner sources. These data add more evidence to our findings on policy and role ambiguity noted above, that if diocesan policies were present, PLCs felt more ambiguity coming from parishioner sources. Here we have found that if PLCs feel that diocesan planning is adequate, then they experience more ambiguity coming from parishioner expectations. Taken together these findings show that if the diocese has adequate planning and policies, then PLCs experience more ambiguity in their relations with their parishioners. Again we would offer this explanation: the more carefully dioceses have thought through and planned out their PLC policies, the more the PLC finds herself caught between diocesan expectations and those of her parishioners, which may be based upon entirely different presumptions, orientations, beliefs and theologies. It is likely that the diocese that has had careful planning and well-spelled-out policies has itself resolved many of the questions with which many parishioners must still be wrestling.

Diocesan planning and diocesan role ambiguity—On the other hand, these data show a reversed pattern when the source of ambiguity is considered to be the diocese. The more inadequate the PLC perceives the diocesan planning, the more her role is ambiguous from the perspective of diocesan expectations. This is consistent with data reported earlier on PLC policies and role ambiguity that showed that when PLC policies were absent or inadequate, more role ambiguity existed. It appears that planning does not always have positive impacts upon the life of the PLC. When things are right with the diocese, things may go wrong with parishioners and vice-versa. Perhaps what is needed is more coordinated planning with the parishes. Even the dioceses in our sample admitted that more education of parishioners needs to take place. It would appear from these data that good planning only at the diocesan level may reduce one source of ambiguity and emotional upset while it creates still another. The concept of role ambiguity would point out to us that expectations must not only be present but they must be consistent from one level of an organization to another. We need to know more about the sets of expectations operating at both diocesan and parish levels and then we need to check them for consistency.

Diocesan planning and the emotional state of the PLC—There is no evidence that if the PLC believes that diocesan planning is inadequate that this translates into either positive or negative emotional states. There is no connection between this belief and the emotional state of the PLC.

Conclusions—We have been able to conclude the following about the perceptions of PLCs and diocesan planning:

- When PLC's see diocesan planning as inadequate, they also feel that PLC-related policies are absent.

- Where diocesan planning is seen as adequate, the PLC sees things as working.

- The more inadequate the diocesan planning the more role ambiguity coming from the diocese.

- The more adequate the diocesan planning the more ambiguity coming from parishioner expectations.

- Inadequacy of diocesan planning does not seem to affect the emotional state of the PLC.

2. Parish Planning

Planning and the presence and adequacy of PLC policy—No relationship was found between adequacy of parish planning and the presence or absence of PLC policies. However, a relationship does exist between parish planning and adequacy of PLC policies. When PLCs believe that parish PLC planning is adequate, they feel that PLC policies are inadequate. While this may appear at first to be a contradiction, it makes sense when one inspects the lists of policies presented to the PLCs. They were asked about the adequacy of diocesan ministries, parish ministries policies, a diocesan PLC plan, a coordinated diocesan/parish PLC policy, diocesan and parish accountability policies and policies dealing with PLC contracts, benefits, contract length and benefits. Most of these are diocesan-level policies. Our data reflects the tension we have also noted in several spots between diocese, parish and PLC. We believe that the PLCs are telling us here that if diocesan planning is adequate, parish planning isn't, and if parish planning is adequate, diocesan planning isn't. The PLC sometimes is caught between these two realities. She may plan carefully with her parish only to find some problems with the diocese. If the diocese has worked out some plans, they may conflict with parish realities.

Parish planning and what is working—As they do with diocesan planning, PLCs are more inclined to say that things are working out in their parish assignment when they think parish planning is adequate. Of the top five things they feel are working with their ministry in the parish (parish acceptance, enabling of the people, adequate authority to do job, people are being served, good relations with parishioners), all either are the same or higher when the PLC says that parish planning is adequate. Our data leads to the more general conclusion that to make things work diocesan and parish planning are important in the mind of the PLC.

Parish planning and role ambiguity—Our data do not support any connection between adequacy of parish planning and role ambiguity coming from diocesan sources. As the level of parish planning would not appear to have anything to do with expectations from the diocese, this is as we would expect it. However, we did find that when parish planning is believed to be adequate, PLCs do experience higher levels of role ambiguity. This may highlight an additional source of problems for the PLC. When planning takes place, new expectations arise, complexity increases, there are more unknowns to deal with and more demands to be met. The more things become institutionalized and publicized in a parish, the more opportunity exists for dissension, conflict and disagreement. While planning may solve many sources of ambiguity, it appears to create others in the process. Thus, as with other data we have presented, planning may be a double-edged sword, solving some problems as it creates others.

Parish planning and the emotional state of the PLC—Inadequate parish PLC planning is a potent source of emotional strain for PLCs. Virtually all of the 16 emotional states presented to the PLCs are more negative when they perceive parish planning to be inadequate. In particular, the two emotional states of feeling unsupported by the bishop and by the priests with whom the PLC works are most related to an inadequate state of parish planning. We have previously found policy absence and inadequacy as well as role ambiguity to be sources of emotional distress to the PLC. To that we add inadequate parish planning.

Conclusions—Our data on the role of parish planning allow us to make the following generalizations:

- When PLCs find their parish planning to be adequate, they nonetheless find PLC policies to be inadequate.

- Where parish planning is seen as adequate, the PLC perceives that things are working out with her PLC ministry in the parish.

- The more adequate the PLC says her parish's planning for PLC work, the more role ambiguity she expresses coming from parish sources.

- When PLCs say their parish planning for PLCs is inadequate they express more negative emotional states.

Some final thoughts on planning and PLC work are in order. The diocesan plan gives a broad picture to the parish and its ministers. Parishes, in planning for their particular local realities, can seem to be much more myopic by comparison. Parishes may be operating on a very inadequate theory of parish. The question for the parish may be how to realize the religious faith community called for in the diocesan plan. The parish must balance the ideal coming from the diocesan plan with the reality of the parish. Parish plans have the potential of making jobs more difficult by increasing the complexities with which one must grapple. The plan may raise all sorts of questions which were formerly left unanswered. The PLC steps into a job that appears to be overwhelming—multiple needs to be met, exhausting tasks—but the authority of the PLC may be circumscribed by the diocese. The parish plan becomes one more set of expectations to be met. Often this leads to conflict for the PLC: to meet the needs of the parish may take her beyond the authority given her by the bishop. The PLC who leads the parish in good form is often asked to add on various deanery and diocesan projects, placing further sets of expectations on her.

3. PLC Formation

PLC formation and policy presence and adequacy—Our data support the notion that the more adequate the PLC says her formation for PLC work has been, the more she feels that PLC policies are both absent and inadequate. This is perhaps the phenomenon of the critical eye of the expert operating. Those PLCs that have had appropriate degree work, courses, workshops, experience in teaching, parish work, training as a pastoral associate, and the like, are more likely to see weaknesses in the present diocesan/parish arrangements for pastoral administration of parishes without resident priests. Likewise, as they better understand the nature of parish life coordination, they perhaps are also critical of the contract, salary and benefits aspects of policy. Also, the better educated a person is the more critical they are of most things. Their superior training and experience gives them more insight into operations and how they deviate from the ideal model. These data indicate that as dioceses and parishes become more familiar with this type of pastoral assignment, they can expect more critical thinking from PLCs concerning existing and needed PLC policies. Of particular note is the fact that the more adequately trained and prepared the PLC feels the more likely she is to feel that the following policies are either absent and inadequate or merely absent:

PLC formation and the emotional state of the PLC—When PLCs admitted that their own formation for PLC work was inadequate, they also admitted to virtually all of the 16 negative emotional states (less supported by bishop and priests, less

Table 2.28
Policies Believed Absent *and* Inadequate
When PLC Formation is Adequate

Parish accountability
Salary
Internship

Policies Believed Absent
When PLC Formation is Adequate

Parish ministries
Diocesan PLC plan
Coordination between parish and diocese

successful, more exhausted, less well received, and so on). In particular, when PLCs felt inadequate in their own formation for the PLC role, they most often expressed the following negative emotional states:

Table 2.29
Emotions Most Prevalent
When PLC Felt Formation To Be Inadequate

Unsuccessful
Not well received
Unaccomplished
Like an outsider

PLC formation and role ambiguity—It would be expected that if a PLC felt that her training and formation were inadequate to handle the PLC job, she would likely express this in the form of role ambiguity. If one feels inadequately prepared one is not as likely to know what is expected, and therefore experience role ambiguity. Our data do confirm this expectation when it comes to role ambiguity coming from parishioner sources. However, a weaker reverse pattern exists when observing role ambiguity coming from the diocese. When the PLC feels inadequate and insecure she also feels she doesn't know what is expected of her from her congregation. On the other hand, when she feels her preparation has been adequate, she feels a certain degree of ambiguity with the diocese. Perhaps this is further evidence in support of the pattern we have noted, in which the PLC finds herself caught between diocese and parish.

What this means is that the adequately prepared PLC feels ambiguity from the diocese when she does not experience ambiguity from the parish. Or she feels ambiguity from the parish when she feels less ambiguity from the diocese. It does appear that education, training and experience play a role in the explanation of the dilemma. If she pleases one level, she offends the other. This suggests that while parishes may be having difficulties with the poorly prepared PLC, dioceses may be having trouble with the more adequately prepared PLC. Is it possible that the adequately prepared PLC is having trouble with inadequately prepared dioceses, but does not have corresponding difficulties with an adequately prepared parish?

Conclusions—Our data on the formation adequacy of the PLC allows us to make the following general conclusions:

- Adequately prepared PLCs find PLC polices either more absent or more inadequate than less adequately prepared PLCs.

- The more inadequate the PLC perceives her formation to be, the more negative emotions she possesses.

- The more adequate the formation of the PLC, the less the role ambiguity from the parish, but the more ambiguity coming from the diocese. Or, the less adequate the formation of the PLC, the more role ambiguity from the parish, but the less ambiguity coming from the diocese.

F. Fulfilled and Unfulfilled Needs of the PLC

1. Fulfilled Needs

The PLCs we studied were asked to list in an open-ended way what needs they felt had been met by the activities performed as a parish life coordinator in their parish. A wide array of needs were expressed. We have summarized the most frequently occurring answers here:

Table 2.30
Personal Needs Fulfilled by PLC Role

Being needed
Sharing life of people
Being in public ministry
Enabling people
Staying active and challenged
Recognizing God in people's lives
Personal spirituality
Forming communities

Other fulfilled needs occurring less frequently are responsibility, self esteem, participating in a new ministry, being a woman in a leadership position, freedom, sacramental preparation of parishioners, teaching, improving physical plant, participating in native liturgy, working with parish council, collaboration, working in a rural setting, being active with the young and having time for one's family.

2. Unfulfilled Needs

While PLCs admitted to a number of needs being fulfilled by being a parish life coordinator, they nonetheless told us of a number of frustrated needs. This list is much more diverse and therefore we will highlight only the top nine that appeared frequently.

Other less commonly occurring responses were lack of spiritual growth in the parish, parish programs not facilitated, lack of staff support, lack of intellectual stimulation, unauthorized to fill the sacramental role, lack of spiritual opportunities, less Eucharist occurring, inability to preach, cultural isolation, marriage being hurt, not teaching and distance to the city.

Table 2.31
Unfulfilled Personal Needs from PLC Role

1. Lack of diocesan support
2. Isolation (social and physical)
3. Lack of resources
4. Treated as unequal
5. Unfulfilled Personal Needs from PLC Role
6. Lack of diocesan support
7. Isolation (social and physical)
8. Lack of resources
9. Treated as unequal
10. Poor relations with priests
11. Lack of collaboration
12. Being unchallenged
13. Lack of professional counseling
14. Not enough time—Poor relations with priests
15. Lack of collaboration
16. Being unchallenged
17. Lack of professional counseling
18. Not enough time

G. The Formation of the PLC

Our questionnaire asked PLCs to tell us about their formation or preparation for becoming a parish life coordinator in their parish. We wanted to know both the formal and informal training they had undergone up to that time. We then wanted to know what were the official requirements in terms of formation for the parish life coordinator's position in the parish. Finally, we sought to find out in what ways the PLC has found her formation to be adequate and how she has found it to be inadequate. We start first with the evidence on what formation PLCs have had.

1. Forming the PLC

Formal formation—PLCs say that they have been formed for the role of PLC in five major ways, presented below. One should note that four of these five involve formal educational experiences: i.e., a master's or bachelor's degree, courses and workshops. The fifth, teaching, is probably possible only with degrees in hand. So PLCs are telling us that education is more important in their backgrounds than experience in the field.

Table 2.32
Most Frequent Types of Formal Formation

Master's degree
Courses
Workshops
Bachelor's degree
Teaching

Among the less frequently mentioned types of formation are those that basically involve experiences in the diocese, parish and rural setting. These less frequent types of formal formation included diocesan experience, being a pastoral associate, parish experience, administrative experience, being a deacon, being in rural ministry, being a director of religious education, retreats and certification

So the PLCs are attesting to the preponderance of educational experiences over field experience in their formation backgrounds. We should not conclude from this, however, that they are saying formal education is better than experience, only that they have had more of it in their own backgrounds.

Informal formation—The PLCs were asked to comment not only on their formal formation experiences but there informal

---

Table 2.33
Most Frequent Informal Formation Experiences

Parish ministry
Teaching
Workshops
Administrative experience
Life experience
Religious education
Being a pastoral associate
Working with people

---

ones as well. As would be expected, both the most frequently occurring and the less frequently occurring experiences were from the field, the diocese, the parish and rural ministry.

Also listed, but less frequently, were leadership in a religious community, retreats, rural ministry experience, prayer, diocesan meetings, mentors, chaplaincy, discernment, sacrifice.

2. Formation Requirements of PLCs

PLCs were asked what the parish required of them in the way of formation. Seven requirements came up frequently; another seven appeared less frequently:

Table 2.34
Most Frequent Requirements to Be PLC in the Parish

Unspecified
Experience
Advanced degrees
Parish work
Interview
Application process
Recommendations

Less frequent requirements were decision of the bishop, meet needs of parish, willingness, pastoring charism, spirituality, administrative experience, communication skills.

It will be noticed that of the top seven responses, the most frequently occurring answer was that no requirements were specified. Furthermore, experience, degrees and the hiring process most often describe the steps PLCs have taken to get their jobs.

3. Adequacy of Formation Experiences for Job Requirements

Finally, we inquired of the PLCs in what ways their formation had been adequate or inadequate to meet the requirements for the position of PLC in their parish. Five areas surfaced most frequently. Six others appeared less often.

Table 2.35
Most Frequent Ways Formation Has been Adequate for Job

Provided experience
Gave necessary knowledge
Provided administrative skills
Awareness of parish life
Gave training

The six less frequently listed were knowledge of PLC role, experience from being pastoral associate, how to relate to parish, counseled parishioners, making pastoral decisions, instilled desire.

The most frequent answers reveal that PLCs feel that their backgrounds have provided them with experience, knowledge, skill and awareness.

We also asked the PLCs to state the ways that they felt their formation experiences were inadequate for their roles. They responded with a wide range of answers and we will summarize only the top six answers followed by a sample of the less frequently mentioned answers.

Table 2.36
Most Frequent Ways Formation Is Inadequate
For PLC Role in Parish

No formal preparation
Lacking knowledge of financial affairs of parish
Lacking experience
Doing job not trained for
Lacking knowledge of marriage and family law
Inadequate knowledge of sacraments

The less frequent ways included lack of community-organizing skills, lack of counseling skills, no skills in homiletics, no knowledge of rural culture and inadequate knowledge of Canon Law.

H. What Is Working and What Is Not for the PLC

We end this chapter on the parish life coordinator by presenting what they report is going well or not well in their PLC ministries.

1. What Is Working

There were six most frequent answers to this question.

Table 2.37
Most Frequent Answers
To What Is Working in PLC Role

Parish acceptance
Enabling of the people
Good relations with priests
People are served
Adequate role authority
Parish and staff growth

Also mentioned were presence of liturgy, new parish programs, good cooperation with parish council, CCD is offered, decisions are local, RCIA is present, parish is open.

2. What Isn't Working

Six responses appeared most frequently.

Table 2.38
Most Frequent Responses
To What Isn't Working with PLC Role

Lack of authority
Lack of time
Cultural clashes
Lack of diocesan support
Poor relations with sacramental minister
Lack of priest support

Also mentioned were lack of spiritual life, lack of deanery support, sex prejudice, getting sacramental ministers, not leading Eucharist, cultural clash, reaching the unchurched, relations with parish council.

We will have more to say on what PLCs report is and isn't working in their jobs in the final chapter where we pull together conclusions not only from the PLCs in this chapter, but also from the dioceses and the parishioners in the following chapters. We then will attempt some policy considerations based upon our data. For now we will turn to a presentation of data from our diocesan samples.

3.

Responses from the Dioceses

A. The Sample

The information upon which this diocesan sketch was constructed came from two samples of dioceses: those now using parish life coordinators and those who in our estimation may use them in the future. The first sampling was constructed from a list of 61 dioceses known by IPL to be using PLCs. We wrote to these dioceses, asking for someone with the appropriate knowledge and authority regarding parish life coordinators to answer the questionnaire we had designed. Out of the 54 percent of the dioceses who identified such a person, 33 person said it was the chancellor, 20 percent the director of lay ministry and 15 percent the vicar general. Another 4 percent turned the questionnaire over to the personnel department, the director of pastoral services, a research coordinator or the bishop. Still smaller numbers, 2 percent, placed it with the bishop's assistant, the director of planning, an administrative assistant or the secretary for clergy.

To get a sample of dioceses that do not now have PLCs, we used IPL's judgment and calculations of which dioceses may need PLCs in the next five years using the priest/parish and priest/laity ratios found in Chapter 1, "The Scope and Methods." Of the 34 dioceses chosen by these methods, 28 told us which person filled out the questionnaire. The range of positions was much smaller than the first sample of dioceses: 56 percent identified the chancellor; 13 percent identified the director of pastoral services, the director of lay ministry or the vicar general; 6 percent identified the bishop.

Thus, most of the information about dioceses in this study comes from chancellors, vicars general and directors of lay ministry. This chapter is based on their responses to our questionnaire and the documents they sent us describing their PLC planning and policy.

B. The Use or Potential Use of the PLC

1. Diocesan Plans for Parishes Without Resident Priests

An interesting picture of the dioceses emerges when they are asked if they have any particular plans for parishes without resident priests. Of the dioceses that now have PLCs, 61 percent say they either now have or are planning a policy that would make provision for ministers for parishes without a full-time priest. Nearly half, 46 percent, however, say they are just in the planning stage. So only 15 percent of these dioceses actually have such plans at the moment. By a remarkable contrast, 67 percent of dioceses without PLCs said they do have plans in place. Why the dioceses that already have PLCs seem to be further behind in policy development than those without PLCs is a matter of speculation. It is possible that the dioceses without PLCs have learned from the experience of the dioceses with PLCs and are paving the way with a diocesan plan.

2. Future Use of PLCs by the Dioceses Without PLCs

While all of the dioceses with PLCs have used PLCs at one point in the recent past, only eight dioceses, or 15 percent of the sample, said they do not have any PLCs in place at the moment. Forty-seven percent said they now have from one to three PLCs assigned to parishes throughout the diocese; 28 percent are using four to six; and 9 percent are using seven or more PLCs.

When the dioceses without PLCs were asked if they intended to use PLCs in the next five years, a majority, 54 percent, said that they did intend to do so, 29 percent were uncertain, and only 18 percent said that they were not intending to use PLCs. If one assumes that half of the uncertain dioceses will actually implement the PLC model, then more than seven out of ten (70 percent) of these dioceses will be placing PLCs in parishes. If we also assume that the 61 dioceses that now use PLCs continue the practice, this would mean that over the next five years as many as 77 dioceses will be implementing the PLC model in some way. As we did not incorporate all of the potential dioceses with PLCs in our sampling design, we can assume that even more dioceses may move in this direction in the future.

3. Factors Encouraging/Discouraging the Use of PLCs

The dioceses without PLCs were asked what diocesan and parish factors might encourage or discourage them from moving to the use of PLCs. The leading diocesan factors that would make the dioceses think positively about adopting PLCs are found in the table below.

Table 3.1
Diocesan Factors Encouraging Use of PLCs
(1) Lack of clergy
(2) Degree of lay involvement in the diocese
(3) Geography of the parish
(4) Conserving energy of available priests
(5) Growth of diocese
(6) Special needs of the parish
(7) Ability to find a qualified person

On the other hand, dioceses gave the following reasons to question whether they would go in the direction of the PLC.

Table 3.2
Inhibiting Diocesan Factors

(1) Presence of adequate clergy
(2) Lack of endorsement by priests in diocese
(3) No particular need arises

In our sample, 19 dioceses stated several parish factors that would encourage adoption of the PLC model of alternate pastoring. The responses in order of frequency are found in the table below.

Table 3.3
Parish Factors Encouraging Adoption of PLC

(1) Laity willingness in the parish
(2) Open attitudes in the parishes
(3) Available training for PLCs
(4) Isolation of the parish
(5) Special needs of a parish
(6) Parish resources available
(7) Keeping the parish open

Parish factors inhibiting the move to PLCs are summarized in the next table.

Table 3.4
Parish Factors Inhibiting Adoption of PLCs

(1) Inadequate preparation of people
(2) Consolidation/closing of parishes
(3) Adequate parish personnel
(4) No endorsement by parish priest

4. Settings for the Use of PLCs

Our survey of dioceses asked specifically what types of arrangements they had in mind for parishes without resident priests. Four such settings were suggested: (1) a multiparish priest/pastor—in other words, one priest in charge of more than one parish, (2) a multiparish team—a situation in which pastoral responsibility for two or more parishes is entrusted to a team, (3) a parish cluster—a situation in which each parish retains a separate identity but parishes are yoked for common activities such as religious education, and (4) a parish life coordinator, parish director or pastoral administrator—a nonpriest appointed by the bishop to "pastor" a parish without a resident priest. The range of settings is delineated below.

Table 3.5 Settings for Parishes Without Resident Priests			
	Dioceses Without PLCs (28 Total)	With PLCs (54 Total)	Total
Multiparish priest	17 (63%)	30 (56%)	47
Team	7 (26%)	15 (28%)	22
Clusters11 (41%)	19 (35%)		30
PLCs	11 (41%)	35 (65%)	46

Dioceses with PLCs are somewhat more inclined to use the team (28 percent vs. 26) and, of course, PLCs (65 percent vs. 41). The figure for the dioceses without PLCs should be interpreted to mean that 41 percent of them have an option for PLCs within their plans for parishes without resident priests; they do not, of course, have PLCs now operating. Plans among dioceses without PLCs more often provide for the multiparish priest (63 percent vs. 56 percent) and parish clusters (41 percent vs. 35 percent). With the PLC option eliminated, the dioceses without PLCs therefore have a more limited number of options open to them and could increase their usage of the multiparish team.

A full one third of the dioceses with PLCs said they are using PLCs in the first three settings—that is, with multiparish priests, clusters and teams. This indicates that in about two thirds of the dioceses with PLCs the PLC is serving alone in one or more parishes. Data from the PLC survey discussed in the preceding chapter indicates that about 22 percent of the PLCs are serving two parishes, and 7 percent have 3 parishes. We know from these data that not all PLCs are alone in a parish: about one third are serving in a setting with a multiparish priests, a team or a cluster, and nearly 30 percent of the PLCs have more than one parish.

Realizing the difficulty some respondents may have of pinpointing just what a parish life coordinator is, we allowed some leeway for dioceses to include "informal" PLCs in their responses—meaning any situations where a nonordained person or a deacon is in effect "pastoring" without having been appointed by the bishop. Six of ten (59 percent) of the dioceses with PLCs said they had no informal PLC situations, 7 percent said they occasionally had an informal PLC, 35 percent said they had one or more informal PLCs in their diocese, and 9 percent said they had 4 or more informal PLCs.

Our data reveal that where dioceses with PLCs are using many PLCs (7 or more for the diocese), they deploy them in multiparish priest settings. This would tend to indicate that dioceses use the PLC as "priest-extenders," covering pastoral activities in several parishes by use of a PLC. On the other hand, where dioceses use smaller numbers of PLCs, they more often use them in team and cluster arrangements.

5. Period of Time Dioceses Have Used PLCs

Most of the dioceses (64 percent) that are using PLCs have been doing so for more than five years. Another 26 percent have been using PLCs for three to four years, and only 8 dioceses have taken up this practice just in the last two years. Thus, among this sample there is a large group of "pioneer" dioceses (90 percent) who began using PLCs three years ago or more. This indicates a slowing in the trend toward PLC usage by dioceses in more recent years.

When we asked the "withouts" when they might be getting PLCs in their dioceses, three of them (13 percent) said they already had one or more PLCs, 28 percent said they would within the next two years, 21 percent said that it would be within three to five years, and 38 percent said they were unsure when such a thing would happen. This is some indication that the move to the PLC may be speeding up again, with nearly half of the sample saying they more than likely would adopt PLCs in the next five years. However, there is a sizeable proportion of the sample that just simply does not know if this is the way they will go.

6. Diocesan/Parish Planning for PLCs

The two sets of dioceses were then asked about their methods of planning for PLCs in parishes with pastoring needs. Did they prefer that the parishes in question appeal to the diocese? Or would the diocese initiate the move to a parish life coordinator? Would parishes and the diocese work in tandem to cover pastoring needs by using a parish life coordinator?

The two samples seem to see this process differently. On the one hand, among the "withs," it is the diocese that more often initiates the move to a parish life coordinator. The "withouts" said they would prefer the parish and the diocese work together toward having a PLC fill the pastoring needs of a parish. Perhaps this difference simply reflects the greater amount of experience of the dioceses with PLCs, or perhaps it reflects the desire of the dioceses without PLCs to be more democratic.

For the dioceses that use PLCs and that responded to our survey, 41 percent said that the amount of time from the beginning to the end of planning—from first considering using a PLC to relaying to the parish the decision that it will have a PLC—is from one to six months. Twenty-six percent said that the time is from 7 to 12 months. In other words, 71 percent take a year or less to complete the process. Twenty-two percent said simply that the time varies with each parish. It would seem that dioceses need to begin to plan early on with their parishes to make sure that adequate preparation of the parish can take place. On the other hand, the time must not be too lengthy or the parish will see this as the diocese dragging its feet.

When parishioners were asked how long it was before they got their PLC after being notified that they would, nearly half of the sample (46 percent) said that it was less than one month from the time they first heard that they were getting a PLC to the actual appointment of the PLC. Furthermore, 40 percent of the sample said that they were not adequately prepared by the diocese for a PLC. Granting different perspectives and necessary delays in implementing the PLC decision, dioceses may need to work more carefully with their parishes to avoid the perception that they are doing things too abruptly and without adequately preparing parishioners for this new form of pastoral ministry.

The two sets of dioceses were asked how they went about planning matters concerning PLCs. The "withs" are more inclined to use a PLC committee and the personnel department of the diocese than are "withouts" who might use PLCs in the future. The full breakdown is as follows:

Table 3.6
PLC Planning
Methods of PLC Planning
Used by Dioceses **With** *PLCs*

(1) Personnel departments
(2) Diocesan discussion
(3) Priest councils
(4) General parish communication
(5) Communications with specific parishes
(6) PLC committees

Methods of PLC Planning
Envisioned by Dioceses **Without** *PLCs*

(1) Priest councils
(2) General parish communications
(3) Diocesan discussion
(4) Communications with specific parishes
(5) Personnel departments
(6) Vision statements
(7) Position papers

C. Components of a PLC Policy

The dioceses that are presently installing PLCs in parishes were asked about various components of their policies concerning PLCs. Those dioceses that do not now deploy PLCs but said they might in the future, were asked what components they thought should be a part of any diocesan-wide PLC policy. We have summarized these responses below.

1. Formation

Only 37 percent of the dioceses that have PLCs said they either have or are in the planning stages for a formation program for their PLCs. Thus, 63 percent of the "withs" said they do not envision any such formation program in the future. This probably is because many of these dioceses are tapping into existing programs within the dioceses or are using national programs such as those offered by IPL in Kansas City. By contrast, more of the "withouts" envision some PLC formation program. Only 27 percent said that they do not envision any such program. Such dioceses may simply believe that since they do not have formation programs in their dioceses now, they may have to adopt them in the future, not having had the necessity to consider other sources.

Regardless of the disparity of answers, both sets of dioceses described what components they thought should make up such a formation program. Dioceses with PLCs mentioned an advanced degree, plus other components as follows:

Table 3.7
Top Diocesan Choices for PLC Formation Components
(1) M.A. in pastoral studies (2) Screening (3) Training (4) Lay pastoral ministry program

Other requirements mentioned were experience on a parish staff, a certification program, exposure to an adult leadership process, continuing theological education, and the GRECO Institute.

The diocesan responses parallel the responses of the PLCs themselves when asked to list their formal formation experiences. They mentioned, as we have said: the appropriate master's or bachelor's degree, appropriate course work and workshops. They also mentioned a number of experiences needed to do PLC work effectively: diocesan experience, parish experience, teaching, certification and work in rural ministry.

The dioceses without PLCs were asked to imagine what kinds of formation experiences they wanted for PLCs if and when they adopted such a model. Their responses are as follows:

Table 3.8
Top Choices for Formation by Dioceses without PLCs

(1) Lay leadership training
(2) Degree requirements
(3) Experience
(4) Training in parish administration
(5) Training in leading a parish
(6) Training or courses in theology

So it would seem that the dioceses and the PLCs tend to have a similar set of expectations as to what is necessary to be formed to do parish life coordination: experience in the diocese and parish, ability to lead and administer and appropriate course or degree work.

2. Accountability

The dioceses with PLCs were asked to whom the PLC is accountable. Most dioceses said this is the bishop or the canonical pastor. Others, however, reported it is the vicar general, another PLC, the personnel board of the diocese or the sacramental minister. These same dioceses were asked how they see the PLC role—whether it is an extension of the priest role, an extension of the bishop role or an extension of both the priest and the bishop roles. An overwhelming majority, 98 percent, see it as extending both roles, or at least an extension of the role of the bishop; only a small minority see it as extending the role of the priest-pastor in a parish. Apparently, how one looks at the PLC's role is related to how one looks at the PLC's accountability. Is it related to the shortage of priests, in that the priest extends himself with parish assistants? Or is it related to the bishop's duty to provide pastors for the parishes under his jurisdiction? The vast majority of these dioceses feel comfortable seeing it as an extension of the priest as well as the bishop. Most are less comfortable at seeing it as only an extension of the work of the priest.

3. Advertising

Our study tallied the methods that dioceses use to publicize available PLC positions in parishes. Personal contact, or word of mouth, and the diocesan newspaper were first choices. The complete list of methods is as follows:

Table 3.9
Diocesan Advertising Methods for PLCs

(1) Personal contact (word of mouth)
(2) Diocesan newspaper
(3) Through religious communities
(4) From present pastoral staff of diocese
(5) Resource and referral office
(6) Diocese has not advertised

Other practices mentioned were contacting a pastor, the vicar general's office, the ministry development office, national sources, the personnel director of the diocese, and deacons. It is interesting to note that, as with many secular jobs, "networking"—personal contact and word of mouth play a big role in finding people for a PLC position.

4. Interviewing

We further explored how dioceses interview candidates for this position. Most frequently they are interviewed by the personnel board followed by the bishop. Others may include the vicar general or the pastor. The complete breakdown is as follows:

Table 3.10
Interviewers of Potential PLCs

· (1) Personnel board
(2) Bishop
(3) Vicar general
(4) Pastor of parish in question
(5) Chancellor
(6) Director of ministry

Infrequent responses were the people of the parish, the dean or a certification committee. It should be noted that a number of dioceses did not respond in this area, and thus this is not a comprehensive picture.

5. Hiring

When asked who actually hires a PLC, most dioceses responded that it is the bishop. Others are the vicar general, the parish or the personnel board.

6. Components of a Contract

Nearly two thirds of the dioceses with PLCs said that a specified salary, benefits and contract length are important components of any PLC contract. When the PLCs themselves were asked if their diocese had a PLC contract, the majority, 56 percent, said that it did not; 29 percent of these respondents found this condition to be inadequate, although 21 percent found this to be adequate to their situation. When they were asked about a salary policy, 40 percent said that it was absent in their diocese, with nearly 25 percent adding that this situation was inadequate, while 21 percent found it adequate. Regarding benefits statements, 37 percent said no such statements were present; 12 percent found this to be inadequate, and 32 percent said that this condition was nonetheless adequate. These data seem to indicate that having stated benefits is not as important to the PLCs as some other contract components.

A little more than 50 percent of the dioceses with PLCs believe that the contract should state housing arrangements and the termination conditions for PLCs. The issue of termination of the PLC points to some of the inherent ambiguities of the PLC role. Should the PLC be terminated when a priest becomes available? If the PLC role is seen only as an extension of the bishop's or priest's role, this would seem to be necessary. But those who see this "pastoring" work as a logical extension of Baptism argue that the PLC role is more than merely an extension of the role of the priest. It is a part of the priestly role of the laity and is unrelated to the availability of priests. Thus, the contract should specify the length of a PLC's tenure in the parish.

The above diocesan data on the PLC contract, as well as the data presented by PLCs in the preceding chapter, indicate that components of the contract are highly consequential for the PLC and how she perceives her work. Much of the ambiguity that is found within this role may be less attributable to theology as it is to the fact that dioceses have not institutionalized the PLC role with adequate policies, planning and contracting.

7. Installation

Approximately one half of these dioceses install a PLC into the parish community using some special procedure. The most frequently cited installation is by a visit from the bishop, the local dean or some other representative of the diocese. The complete list of answers is as follows:

Table 3.11
Methods of Installing PLC in Parish

(1) Bishop
(2) Local dean
(3) Vicar general
(4) Former pastor of parish
(5) Parish community
(6) Public ceremony
(7) Priest moderator
(8) Diocesan director of ministry

The most commonly mentioned officiator at installation ceremonies was the bishop, followed by the dean or the vicar general. The director of ministry and the former or exiting pastor were also mentioned.

8. Internship

Only 20 percent of the dioceses using PLCs provided an internship for their PLCs. This is an exact mirror of the responses from the PLCs themselves, 20 percent of whom said that there is an internship present in their diocese. The majority, 80 percent, also said that this situation was inadequate or merely adequate. Dioceses would do well to plan for a routine internship of up to a year before the PLC is officially installed in the parish. Other data from the PLCs indicate that of all the various components of a diocesan policy concerning PLCs they view the lack of an internship component as among the most serious defect in diocesan planning.

9. Diocesan/PLC Affiliation

When asked how the PLC is included in diocesan affiliation, the most common answers given by the dioceses with PLCs were attendance at meetings, plus reception of correspondence, as follows:

Table 3.12
Types of PLC/Diocesan Affiliation

(1) Regional pastors' meetings
(2) Deanery meetings
(3) PLC meetings
(4) Vicariate meetings
(5) Diocesan correspondence directed to pastors
(6) Other diocesan meetings

Also mentioned were attendance at pastor- or priest-sponsored events, offering of diocesan financial assistance for study, various committee meetings, meetings with the bishop, clergy continuing education and use of diocesan services.

10. Financial Assistance

Only 6 percent of the dioceses with PLCs said they give financial assistance to the PLC. However, 35 percent said they give help in some circumstances, such as through the Extension Society, automobile purchase assistance, missionary parish assistance, housing or one-year stipends. Nonetheless, 60 percent of the sample give no financial assistance at all.

11. Appropriate Activities

Dioceses with PLCs were asked to rank five areas of "pastoring" activities for the PLC appointed to a parish. The results, ranked from most appropriate on the top to least appropriate at the bottom, are as follows:

(1)   Community life—Visiting the sick and elderly, promoting family, community building, coordinating volunteers, RCIA, ecumenical contact, hospitality.

(2)   Administration—General parish administration, control of finances, parish communications, conflict management.

(3)   Worship—Communion services, prayer services and groups, liturgical education, sacramental preparation, funeral rites, Liturgy of the Word, weekend liturgies, preaching, Sunday reflections, Sunday Eucharist in absence of a priest.

(4)   Outreach—Evangelization, home visitations, help to needy and powerless, social justice education, team forming, crisis intervention.

(5)   Proclamation and teaching—Religious education (CCD), RCIA, non-Eucharistic preaching, announcements, mass media ministry, Bible study, weddings, wakes.

It is interesting to point out that dioceses rank outreach and proclamation as the least appropriate, whereas administration and community life are seen as more appropriate. Perhaps this is because the outreach and proclamation activities are seen as closer to the traditional priest role, while administration and community affairs come closer to traditional lay roles.

12. Evaluation

Sixty-one percent of the Dioceses with PLCs said that they have an evaluation process for the PLC, 78 percent of which evaluate the PLC at least once a year and 18 percent evaluate the PLC than once a year. Only 21 percent less often than once a year.

A number of persons are involved in the evaluation, and no general pattern prevails. The most commonly mentioned persons are the bishop, the vicar general, the diocesan director of ministry, the canonical pastor or the parish pastoral council.

Others mentioned were the priest evaluation team, a parish life coordinator committee or the personnel director of the diocese.

13. Ideal Policy Components for Dioceses without PLCs

The dioceses that presently do not have PLCs were asked to speculate what a PLC policy should encompass. The top answers were a list of qualifications, a job description, standardized compensation, academic credentials, provision for due process and accountability. Less frequently mentioned were that the PLC should: be an employee of the diocese, be familiar with the diocese, be committed to serving people in a parish, have pastoral skills and have a theology background. This corresponds roughly to PLCs' own descriptions of policy requirements.

D. What Is Working and What Is Not Working About the PLC

1. What Is Working

From having adopted and worked with the PLC model for some years, dioceses presented a rather long list of things they feel are working. The most frequently mentioned bright spots in this innovative form of "pastoring" were:

Table 3.13
Successes with the PLC Model

(1) Priest-PLC relationships are good
(2) PLCs are effective in this ministry
(3) Parishes are adequately prepared
(4) Parishes are open and functioning
(5) Someone is in charge in the parish
(6) The parish has been empowered
(7) The PLC is included in diocesan functioning

Less frequently mentioned successes were that the work of the PLC is rewarding, the PLC is responsible to the bishop, and the PLC selection process is successful.

The dioceses appear to be proud of what they have accomplished and are working to alleviate some of the problems which we have summarized below.

2. What Is Not Working

The most frequently mentioned problem areas with the diocesan use of PLCs are the following:

Table 3.14
Challenges with the PLC Model
(1) Parishioners are reluctant to accept this form of ministry
(2) Diocesan priests do not accept this form of ministry
(3) Sufficient parishioner education on the PLC role is lacking
(4) There is ambiguity in the PLC role
(5) The formation of the PLC has been inadequate

Areas also not working well but less frequently mentioned are the administrative aspects of the PLC role, inadequate PLC compensation, inadequate hiring process, poor self esteem among priests working with PLCs, inadequate diocesan funding of PLCs, and sacramental life of the parish is split between the priest and the PLC.

We shall return to these successes and challenges in the closing chapter of this book where we pull together the perspectives not only of the dioceses, but the PLCs and the parishioners also. We finish this chapter with a look at what dioceses think might be their alternatives to the PLC model of parish ministry .

E. Diocesan Alternatives to the PLC

Both sets of dioceses were asked, in light of a shortage or potential shortage of ordained priests to pastor their parishes, what alternatives to the PLC approach they believe to exist. The most frequently mentioned options were:

Table 3.15
Alternatives to PLC Model

(1) Consolidation/closing of parishes
(2) Multiparish teams
(3) Multiparish priests
(4) Multiparish clusters

Less frequently mentioned were:

(5) Lay ministry expansion
(6) Use of married priests
(7) Use of deacons
(8) Importing clergy
(9) Vocations recruiting.

Dean Hoge, in his book *Future of Catholic Leadership*, weighs the pros and cons of each of these. He concludes that the most viable option open today to the Church in the U.S. is the fifth mentioned above—expanding lay ministry. These dioceses should take heart in Hoge's work because that is exactly what they are doing. They are presently using the first four options listed, plus using deacons and importing clergy, with or without the PLC. Hoge does not feel that vocations recruiting offers a realistic solution to the growing problem. In effect, these dioceses are saying there is no one other realistic alternative open to them at this time.

It is not known from our study if any of the dioceses with PLCs intend to downplay or eliminate the PLC model and play up any of the other options. Comparative data on the two sets of dioceses indicate that the dioceses with PLCs are a little more inclined to see the consolidation or closing of a parish as an option open to them. We also cannot know how many of the dioceses without PLCs that said they are going to adopt the PLC model will actually do so. It would seem reasonable that both sets of dioceses will continue or start to use the PLC model, according to their circumstances, in addition to various of the other options listed above.

F. Summary

The following is a summary of the more consequential findings among the diocesan responses:

- While our research on the PLCs and parishes shows the great importance of a diocesan plan for parishes without resident priests, nearly one third of both samples of dioceses do not have such plans at this time.

- Within the next five years as many as 77 dioceses nationwide could be using the PLC model.

- While two thirds of dioceses use a PLC in one or several parishes where they serve alone, fully one third of dioceses use PLCs in multiparish priests, teams and cluster settings.

- Dioceses that deploy the largest number of PLCs are using them mostly in multiparish priest settings.

- Nearly 40 percent of the dioceses with PLCs said they use PLCs in an informal way without official appointment by the bishop.

- While a slowing of appointments of new PLCs is evident in the last several years, there is reason to believe that another round of PLC deployment is likely to take place in the near future.

- Dioceses and parishioners do not perceive the time it takes to deploy a PLC in a parish in the same way. Parishioners are likely to feel that the PLC was sprung upon them without adequate diocesan preparation.

- The overwhelming number of dioceses see PLC work as both priest-extender and bishop-extender work.

- Sizeable minorities of PLCs find diocesan contract components either absent or inadequate.

- About half of all dioceses do not have an installation ceremony for the PLC.

- Only one in five dioceses makes provision for internships for their PLCs.

- Only about 6 percent of dioceses make financial arrangements with their PLCs.

- Dioceses tend to see outreach and proclamation and teaching functions of the PLC as less appropriate activities than community life and administrative functions.

- Dioceses find the following problematic with the PLC model: reluctance of parishioners to accept the PLC, lack of parishioner education about PLCs, lack of acceptance of this kind of ministry by diocesan priests, ambiguity of the PLC role and inadequate formation of the PLC.

- Dioceses find the following successes with the PLC model: good PLC/priest relationship, an effective ministry, adequately prepared parishes, parishes open and functioning, someone in charge in the parish, empowerment of the parish.

4.

Responses from Parishioners
With PLCs

A. Parishioner Sample and Demographic Profile

The Sample—Parishes who now have parish life coordinators were chosen for this study in a random systematic way. Every nth PLC whom we queried was also asked if her parish community would be willing to participate in the study. A total of 15 PLCs volunteered their parishes and sent us their parish rosters. A total of 687 parishioners were mailed questionnaires.

The 15 parishes were distributed geographically thus:

(1) South Central	2 parishes
(2) Midwest	8 parishes
(3) Mid-central	4 parishes
(4) West	1 parish

Out of the original 687, a total of 385 useable questionnaires, or 59 percent of the original sample, were returned. It
is from these that the data in this chapter are drawn. As the
15 parishes were selected in a representative fashion, it is felt
that a high level of generalization from these results can be
applied to Catholic parishioners in the U.S. who have parish
life coordinators. It is not known, however, how comparable
these parishioners are to the parishioners who have priest-pastors but may be heading toward a part-time priest. We will
compare and contrast these two sets of parishioners using the
sample results we received. Because of the judgmental
method of selecting parishes without PLCs, which we will
study in the next chapter, it is not known if the sample results
are representative of the whole population of parishioners
without PLCs.

Demographic Profile—It should be noted that 66 percent of the
parishioners returning useable questionnaires were female, creating a possible bias.

Parishioners with no PLCs are somewhat younger than
parishioners without PLCs. We found that 36 percent were
under the age of 40, and 43 percent were over 50. Of parishioners without PLCs, 34 percent were under 40 and 47 percent
were over 50. Nonetheless the two samples overall are about
the same average age.

The parishioners with PLCs more than likely are married
(77 percent vs. 67 percent), are married women (53 percent vs.
37 percent) and have been married 15 years or less. They are
underrepresented in the single, divorced and widowed categories. While the number of children is nearly identical in both
samples, more PLC parishioners have only one child.

On the two indicators of social class used in our study—
the occupational and educational status of respondent and
spouse—parishioners with PLCs generally represent higher occupational and educational levels than the parishioners without PLCs.

Both samples have identically the same percentages that
say they are members of parish communities (71 percent).

In conclusion then, the parishioner-with-PLC sample is
overrepresented with married females who have been married

for fewer years and who are higher in social status than parishioners without PLCs. To the degree that these factors correlate with any of the other factors studied, they could represent biases in some of the responses.

B. Who Is Qualified to Pastor the Parish

In both samples, we asked parishioners whom they felt would be qualified to "pastor" their parish in the event a full-time priest was not available. They were given the traditional choice of a part-time priest, followed by less traditional choices of a deacon or a religious. Finally, we gave them the least traditional choices of all: lay man, lay woman or a married couple.

Parishioners in both samples made a sharp distinction in the qualifications between the religiously trained or ordained person and the more ordinary lay person, although they were slightly more approving of a lay man rather than a lay woman or a married couple, as the table below indicates. It should also be noted from the table that parishioners with PLCs are more tolerant of each category of pastor-substitute than are parishioners with PLCs. Both samples are about equal in their acceptance of the ordained.

Table 4.1 Who Is Qualified to Pastor the Parish			
Person Qualified to "Pastor" Parish	Without PLC	With PLC	Difference
Part-time priest	91%	93%	2%
Deacon	82	83	1
Religious	79	88	9
Lay man	46	50	4
Lay woman	42	48	6
Married couple	40	45	5

Why parishioners with PLCs are more accepting of non-traditional choices is a matter of speculation. Perhaps having had the experience of a PLC—whom it should be recalled can be a sister, brother or lay person—is sufficient to make them more open-minded toward alternate types of pastoring. Furthermore, 23 percent of the sample says they have had two or more PLCs up to this time. These data suggest that when parishioners are faced with the inevitability of nontraditional "pastors" they are likely to resolve whatever prejudice they had before the new "pastor" arrives. As with all other data discussed in this section, the fact that the parishioners with PLCs are of a somewhat higher social status and that more are female may contribute to their greater tolerance.

We now look at some of the correlates of this tolerance by dividing the potential causal factors into three categories: diocesan, parish and parishioner. It must be kept in mind, however, that the data represent parishioner *perceptions* of how the diocese, parish and parishioners operate.

1. Diocesan Factors

Existence of a diocesan plan to appoint PLCs in the future— From the total sample 23 percent said they were aware the diocese had a plan to appoint PLCs in their parishes in the future, 7 percent said they knew of no such plan, and the other 70 percent said they didn't know if there was or was not such a plan. Thus, the vast majority of parishioners are not aware of any plans the dioceses have to appoint PLCs, even though two thirds of the dioceses have such plans, as reported in Chapter III. It is apparent, then, that parishioners are generally uninformed about their diocese's plans in this matter.

One item of note here is that parishioners who say they do not know of such plans are more likely to feel that all nonpriest individuals are qualified to pastor their parishes than are those parishioners who are aware of such plans.

Selection of one's own parish—Parishioners seem to be generally unaware whether their own parish has actually been selected by the diocese to receive a PLC. Fully 73 percent of the sample said that they did not know if their parish was selected according to some diocesan PLC plan for parishes. Both this and the finding noted above indicate that dioceses need to better communicate their planning to parishioners.

Asked to state specifically why their parish was selected for a PLC, the parishioners gave the following answers:

Table 4.2
Parishioners' Reasons Why Parish Selected for PLC

(1) Lack of priests
(2) Lack of a full-time priest
(3) Small size of parish
(4) Necessity
(5) Parish location
(6) Not aware of reason

Those parishioners who said they weren't selected in this plan or who said they don't know if they were selected were more inclined to feel that all nonpriest individuals are qualified to pastor in their parishes. The interpretation of this significant statistic is not clear. Perhaps the sample contained a number of parishes in which PLCs pioneered this new style of pastoring before dioceses had constructed anything so formal as a parish PLC plan. Having a PLC has made these parishioners accept nontraditional substitutes for full-time pastors.

Length of time before getting PLC—Nearly half of the sample (46 percent) said that it was less than one month from the time they first heard that they were getting a PLC until the PLC was appointed. How they first found out about the appointment is described below:

Table 4.3
How Parishioners Heard They Were Getting a PLC

(1) Announced at Mass
(2) Told by bishop
(3) Told by pastor
(4) Heard from parishioners

The speed and manner of presentation of these decisions raises the issue of how dioceses need to plan with their parishes in preparing them for a PLC. The data make one wonder if several weeks are enough warning and preparation time for a parish. While 60 percent of the sample feel that their diocese adequately prepared them for their PLC, fully 40 percent felt unprepared for what happened to them. Some would argue that a year of internship is not only necessary for the PLC, it is necessary for the parish as well.

Another finding also supports the need for better planning. Parishioners who say they had more than a month's notice of the PLC's arrival are also more likely to approve of PLCs. While it is possible that these parishioners who are more informed may be the better educated and therefore already more tolerant, as we have seen, these parishioners still may have benefitted from a more adequate preparation time.

Summary—A parishioner's awareness of diocesan plans is important to his or her attitude concerning who is qualified to pastor the parish in the absence of a resident priest. Those who say they are not aware of a PLC plan for their parish at the diocesan level, those who say either that they weren't selected or that they are not aware that they were selected, and, finally, those who say they had more than a month's notice before the PLC was installed in their parish are more likely to say that all the persons presented to them as potential pastors are qualified to do so in their parish.

2. Parish Factors

History of the parish without a resident priest—In our sample, 43 percent of parishioners said that their parish had been without a resident priest at some time in the past. Another 42 percent said that they had never been without a priest. Only 16 percent said that they did not know. This is significant in that parishioners who say they have been without a resident priest or who don't know if they have are more inclined to accept the complete list of "pastor" choices. Perhaps those who have not had a priest in the past have become more mentally prepared to accept lay persons in "pastoring" work. In addition, many small or rural parishes have had to make do with volunteer help for long periods in their history. Lay men and women and married couples have already been doing much of the "pastoring" work within these parishes. When asked, parishioners from these circumstances are more likely to say they'd now accept such persons as "pastors." The same line of thinking may go into the equally accepting attitude of those who do not know if they have been without a priest.

Number of PLCs in parish history—A great majority of parishioners, 77 percent, report that they have had only one PLC. The remaining 23 percent have had two or more. These latter are more inclined to say that all of the nontraditional candidates are qualified to pastor—a testimony, perhaps, to the success of the PLC. Parishioners in effect are saying that they have liked or had a good experience with their PLCs and that therefore other lay persons should also be qualified to "pastor" their parishes. A parish that has experienced this type of pastoring prepares its parishioners to accept others like them.

Priest/PLC relations—The vast majority of parishioners—91 percent—responded that there have been good relations between their PLC and the priest appointed to take care of the pastoral oversight and sacramental needs of the parish. When parishioners feel that relations between the priest and the PLC have been good they also feel that from our list of pastor candidates the part-time priest or the religious would be the most qualified. Conversely, the minority of parishioners who perceive that the priest/PLC relations have been poor are also more likely to feel that the lay man, lay woman or married couple would also be qualified. Depending upon which side of the priest-PLC relation one focuses, several interpretations of these findings are possible. The parishioners who blame the PLC for the poor relationship may be saying that they want a nun or a priest only. However, if they feel that the priest has been the major cause of the bad blood, then they may prefer lay persons.

Summary—We have isolated three parish factors that seem to determine why some parishioners feel nontraditional candidates are qualified to pastor their parish in the absence of a full-time priest: (1) those who know or think maybe their parish has been without a resident priest in the past, (2) those who have had more than one PLC in their parish, and (3) those who think the relationship between the PLC and the supervising priest have been poor. These data give the distinct impression that a history of having PLCs and not having priests help form parishioners' attitudes about emerging models of pastoral ministry. The impact of negative relations between priests and PLCs is still a matter of speculation.

3. Parishioner Factors

Parishioner support for the PLC—Parishioners clearly say that they support their PLCs—96 percent responded that are supportive or very supportive. It is possible that a bias entered from the way in which the parishioner sample was selected for the study. Parishioners could not be part of the study unless the PLC gave us her parish list. It is possible that only those PLCs who have good relations with their parishioners chose to submit parish lists. The support that a parishioner gives to his or her parish PLC is an important factor in determining their attitude about the qualifications of other lay persons to pastor their parish. Those who are the most supportive of their PLC are also most supportive of nonpriests pastoring their parish. However, those who are the least supportive of the PLC are those who lean toward the part-time priest as the one qualified to pastor their parish when they have no full-time priest. Nonetheless, the vast majority of the sample are supportive and are open to lay persons pastoring in their parishes.

Parishioner openness to PLC—Parishioners were asked to recall how open they were to the idea of a PLC when they first heard about getting one and how they now felt after one had been working in the parish. Fully 72 percent said that they were open or very open upon hearing of the idea. After experiencing a "real live" PLC, the acceptance increases—89 percent said they were open or very open. These figures demonstrate a high level of initial support that broadens into an even higher level upon experience. Furthermore, those parishioners that have been the most open all along are those who are most accepting of a nonpriest as "pastor" of their parish.

So we have abundant evidence here that PLC parishioners not only accept their PLCs but are most willing to accept nonpriests as "pastors."

Demographic profile of accepting parishioner—The parishioners in our sample who are most accepting of nonpriests as "pastor" of their parish came from the following categories: Catholic educated, married women, single men, divorced and remarried, widowed, young and not members of a parish community.

Summary—We have demonstrated based upon our data that certain diocesan, parish and parishioner factors seem to impinge upon parishioners' attitudes concerning who is qualified to pastor their parish if there is no full-time priest. We have been presuming all along that those parishioners who would accept only a part-time priest—regarded as a traditional choice—are different types of individuals from those who would also accept a married couple or a lay person—whom we regard as nontraditional. The following is a synopsis of

---

Table 4.4
Strongest Factors Affecting Parishioners' Acceptance of the Nontraditional Candidate

Diocesan Factors

   (1) Not aware of any diocesan plan for a PLC for their parish.
   (2) Not selected or don't know if they were selected by this plan.
   (3) One month's notice or longer of the appointment of a PLC.

Parish Factors

   (1) Know or are unsure if their parish has ever been without a resident priest.
   (2) Have had numerous PLCs in the past.
   (3) Think relations between PLC and priest have been poor.

Parishioner Factors

   (1) Have been supportive of the PLC.
   (2) Were open to the idea of a PLC in their parish both before and after the appointment.
   (3) Have Catholic high school and college education.
   (4) Are married women or single men
   (5) Are divorced and remarried or widowed.
   (6) Are young.
   (7) Are not members of a parish community.

the strongest factors affecting parishioners' acceptance of the nontraditional candidate.

C. Eight Roles Appropriate for the Laity

1. Parish Factors

Parishioners were asked what kinds of Church roles they thought were appropriate for lay persons like themselves. We presented eight possible roles that were not expected roles such as Eucharistic minister, cantor or lector, but nontraditional roles many of which normally are relegated to a full-time priest. The roles presented, shown below, resemble the job description of the parish life coordinator. We wanted information on how tolerant lay persons are of other lay persons doing the things that PLCs do.

Table 4.5
Appropriate Roles for the Laity

(1) Pastoral administrator
(2) Planning liturgies
(3) Giving homilies
(4) Counseling parishioners
(5) Visiting the sick and elderly
(6) Conducting certain services
(7) Conducting Communion services
(8) Preparing parishioners for sacraments

The eight activities can be divided roughly into (1) things more traditionally relegated to the priest such as pastoral administration, giving homilies, counseling parishioners, conducting services and Communion services, and (2) things somewhat more appropriate for lay persons, such as visiting the sick and elderly, planning liturgies, and sacramental preparation of parishioners. Parishioners were given the option of evaluating these roles in each of two imaginary scenarios. In the first, their parish has a full-time priest. In the second, their parish will not have a full-time priest in the future.

The following are some correlates of whether parishioners feel that these roles are appropriate for lay persons.

History of parish without a full-time priest—Under the first scenario, having a full-time priest, no relationship emerges between the scenario and reaction to the eight roles. In the second scenario, imagining their parish without a resident priest, parishioners who actually have been without a resident priest were more likely to find all the eight roles more appropriate than those parishioners who have not had the experience of being without a resident priest. This was expected. The data show how the absence of a full-time priest has certain anticipatory effects upon parishioners.

Number of PLCs in the parish—Parishioners who have had two or more PLCs find the lay roles appropriate under both scenarios.

Conclusions—As with the analysis of parishioner acceptance of nontraditional "pastors," we again find that such parish factors as the experience of more than one PLC in the parish and being without a resident priest lead to a greater openness of attitude toward lay roles. The experiences apparently broaden the parishioners' outlook on the laity and various "pastoring" activities.

2. Parishioner Factors

Parishioner's evaluation of the PLC—In general, there is a connection between how a parishioner evaluates the PLC and how that parishioner feels about the eight nontraditional roles for the laity. One would speculate that if a person thought their PLC was doing a good or bad job, this might color their appraisal of these types of activities for other lay persons.

It appears from the data that the relationship depends on which type of role is being considered. It will be recalled that the eight activities can be divided roughly into those traditionally relegated to priests and those that have always had some participation by laity. The data reveal that if the parishioner's evaluation of the PLC is good then that parishioner has no problem seeing laity in those roles more traditionally given to priests. If the parishioner judges the PLC's performance to be poor, however, then he or she will limit lay roles to the ones more traditional for the laity. In other words, when the PLC performs the more priestly roles well, this performance influences parishioners' approval of these roles for other lay persons. This would seem to indicate the crucial importance of the PLC doing well when she administers the parish, gives homilies, counsels and conducts various services. The PLC that does well is "breaking ground" for other lay persons to do the same.

Parishioner openness to the PLC—Parishioners who are presently open to their PLC are also the ones most likely to find the eight roles appropriate. It is a stronger acceptance than when the PLC was announced and accepted but had not yet started working. It is the strongest under the second scenario, imagining the parish without a resident priest in the future. These findings all seem consistent with other findings in that those who are open to the idea of a PLC are also open to seeing other lay persons doing similar things.

Qualifications of potential pastors—A significant association exists between accepting nontraditional candidates to "pastor" one's parish and believing that all the eight roles are appropriate. Again these results are most significant under the conditions of the second scenario. This finding is also consistent with other findings in so far as nontraditional candidates are seen as qualified to do nontraditional activities.

D. Personal Interest and Training in the Eight Lay Roles

We now look at the factors that influence the parishioner's interest in the eight lay roles. For a parishioner to say that he or she regards some or all of the roles as appropriate for a lay person does not translate automatically that that person is personally interested in doing these activities. We wanted to see how many of these same parishioners would say they were personally interested in these various roles.

1. Parish Factors

No resident priest—The parishioner who says the parish has been without a resident priest in the past is also more likely to say that he or she is personally interested in conducting certain services, giving homilies, visiting the sick or performing any one of the other eight lay roles presented to them in this study. When comparing both parishioner samples, parishioners with PLCs are more inclined to be interested in doing one or more of the roles. The experience of being without a resident priest apparently has so impressed the parishioner that he or she is willing to assume a wide variety of nontraditional parish activities to keep the parish going.

Number of PLCs in parish history—Consistent with other findings reported earlier, those parishioners that have had two or more PLCs are more open to actually doing one or more of the eight lay roles. It could be a phenomenon of modelling, in that as parishioners see a counterpart in nontraditional "pastoring" roles they become inspired to do the same.

2. Parishioner Factors

Evaluation of the PLC—The parishioners were asked to evaluate their PLC in seven different areas: (1) forming the parish into a ministering community, (2) enabling individuals and groups to take leadership in ministry, (3) liturgical ministry, (4) educational ministry, (5) administration, (6) ministering to people in crisis, and (7) diocesan involvement. These evaluations also influenced parishioners' interest in the eight roles. They showed more interest in the roles when they felt their PLC was not doing well in community building, leadership, education and diocesan relations. They also showed more interest when they gave positive marks to their PLC in liturgy, administration and crisis intervention.

Openness to the PLC—When parishioners report being open to their PLCS both formerly and now, they are also interested in all eight lay roles. Again, these findings are consistent with others presented earlier.

Qualifications of potential pastors—Regarding nontraditional candidates—lay men and women and married couples as well as religious and deacons—as qualified to pastor one's parish is related to being interested in all of the eight roles. An interesting finding is that when those in our sample feel a part-time priest would not be qualified they show an interest in the eight roles. This pattern shows up on this variable sufficiently often to lead one to believe that some Catholics would just as soon see lay persons pastoring as a part-time priest.

Demographic characteristics of the parishioners—Those most likely to say they are interested in performing one or more of the roles come from the following categories: married men and women, females, middle-aged, the divorced and now single, the never-married and those not belonging to a parish community. Very similar results were found when the factors were correlated with a willingness to be trained for the eight roles. The slightly different demographic profile includes married men and women, females, middle-aged, divorced, married for a moderate number of years and not part of a parish community.

E. The Parishioner's Evaluation of the PLC

As we have mentioned, parishioners were given seven areas in which to evaluate the job their PLC was doing in their parish. The areas and the percent of negative evaluations— very poor, poor or adequate—are given below in rank order, the most negatively evaluated activities at the top:

Table 4.6 Areas of Evaluation		
(1) Forming the parish into a community	20%	(Most negative)
(2) Enabling leadership in parish	19	
(3) Educational ministry	16	
(4) Crisis ministry	15	
(5) Parish administration	14	
(6) Liturgical ministry	11	
(7) Diocesan involvement	11	(Least negative)

It will be noted that the PLCs are given higher marks on the more routine tasks of the parish such as liturgy, administration and diocesan involvement, whereas the areas requiring more skills in human relations such as forming community and leadership are rated lower. Nonetheless, it is quite an accomplishment for these persons to enter into a parish in such a pioneering fashion and receive such high evaluations. At most, two out of ten parishioners express discontent with the performance of their PLC.

We now present the diocesan, parish and parishioner correlates of these PLC evaluations.

1. Diocesan Factors

Selection of the parish for a PLC by diocesan plan—When parishioners say that their parish was not selected to have a PLC in some kind of diocesan plan, they also are likely to give the PLC the poorest evaluations on each of the areas of the evaluation. The explanation may be traced to the conditions under which the PLC began her ministry in those dioceses where there is no PLC. For example, some probably just "fell into" the job after taking over from a sick or recently deceased priest or after starting at the parish to teach religion. Others may have become PLCs under very irregular circumstances. Parishioners may be showing some hostility toward the diocese for allowing their parish to be handled in this fashion and venting their anger on the PLC. Perhaps parishioners are simply saying that selection of a PLC without some guiding rationale does not lead to a good parish situation.

Time before PLC appointment to the parish—One insight into parishioners' negative assessment of their PLC comes from data that reveal that those parishioners who say their parish was given less than a month's notice before receiving their PLC are the same parishioners who give their PLC bad marks on the criteria in the survey. If the PLC mode of pastoring "just evolved" or was thrust upon the parish without adequate preparation, then they may feel negatively toward their PLC.

Adequacy of diocesan preparation for the PLC—Further support for our argument is found in the data that show that when parishioners feel that the diocese either left them unprepared or very unprepared for a PLC they also evaluate their PLC more negatively. While 60 percent of the parishioners in the sample of PLC parishioners said they felt their dioceses prepared them well for their PLC, nearly 40 percent felt that their dioceses did not.

Conclusions—Although the vast majority of parishioners evaluate their PLCs highly, a small proportion of parishioners rank them negatively, partly because of actions on the part of the diocese. When dioceses appoint PLCs without a plan, when they do it too quickly or when they prepare parishioners inadequately for such an experience they either end up with ineffective PLCs or unhappy parishioners.

2. Parish Factors

Adequacy of priest/PLC relations—When parishioners perceive that the relations between their PLC and the priests who serve the parish are poor, they also tend to rate their PLC more negatively than when they find the priest/PLC relations to be good. This is evidence that parishioners may hold the PLC more responsible for the poor relations than they do the priest. While 91 percent of the sample say they believe there are good to very good relations between the PLC and the priest, the remaining who hold a negative view of this relationship seem to hold the PLC accountable. Chapter 2 explores the relations between the PLC, the canonical priest and the sacramental minister in greater detail.

3. Parishioner Factors

Openness of the parishioner to the PLC—Parishioners who say they were formerly closed to the idea of a PLC are inclined to give negative evaluations to their PLC. Those who say they have remained closed are even more likely to give their PLC poor marks.

Support of the PLC—As one would expect, those who give low support to the PLC are also the ones who give the PLC a low evaluation.

Qualifications of pastor candidates—The relationship between regarding nontraditional candidates as qualified to be pastors and giving the PLC a high evaluation is weak and statistically insignificant.

Demographic characteristics of the parishioner—Those parishioners most likely to give the PLC a negative evaluation come from the following categories: better educated, higher status jobs, married men and women, single men, male, married for fewer years, and middle age.

F. Summary

The following is a summary of the conclusive findings from the survey of parishioners with PLCs:

- Parishioners are overwhelmingly accepting of their PLCs. While they may have been open to the idea of the PLC in the first place, they are now more supportive of her than ever. They give their PLCs very high evaluations in most areas of their work.

- This high acceptance of the PLC seems to be associated with and even contributes to a general parishioner acceptance of nonpriests as pastors of their parishes. Sizeable percentages of these parishioners are willing to accept not only a deacon or a sister as pastor, but also a lay man, lay woman or married couple. The experience of having a PLC seems to help these parishioners accept these nonpriest pastors more so than the sample of parishioners we that still have priest-pastors.

- Acceptance of PLCs is related to the manner in which the diocese manages PLC assignments in parishes, such as making PLC plans known to parishioners, selecting parishes according to this plan and giving parishes adequate time to prepare for their PLCs.

- Parish history is also related to parishioner acceptance. Having been without a resident priest in the past, having experienced more than one PLC and having witnessed a poor relation between the priest and the PLC are all contributing factors.

- Catholics who were open to the idea of a PLC in the first place and who remain supportive of their PLC are more likely to have tolerant attitudes toward the ministry.

- These accepting parishioners show strong approval of certain nontraditional roles for lay persons in general, and high percentages are interested in these parish roles themselves, many to the point of saying they would seek training if it were available to them.

- For parishioners who were at first closed to the idea, having a successful PLC may help reduce their objections. In a diocese and parish that have clearly endorsed the PLC model, the parishioner must deal with the conflict between their dislike of the model and the inevitability that the parish will have it. This mental struggle may be alleviated after time and experience. Our data would seem to indicate that much change in attitude has taken place among parishioners. While some persons by nature are already disposed to change, others need help in accepting change. A small minority of Catholics will never accept this new form of ministry.

Based on these data we may conclude that the PLC model is working well in the parishes that have PLCs. This is not to say that there are no problem areas. We will elaborate upon the successes and failures in the final chapter of this book.

5.

Responses from Parishioners Without PLCs

A. Parishioner Sample and Demographic Profile

The Sample—Parishes without parish life coordinators were chosen to be in the study's sample according to two conditions: (1) their bishop felt that the parish may need a parish life coordinator in the near future and (2) the priest-pastor of such a parish was willing to send a roster of his parishioners to be included in the IPL study. A total of six parishes met these conditions. Although other names were submitted by various bishops from many parts of the country, their pastors declined to participate.

This is how the six parishes were distributed geographically:

Midwest	2 parishes
Mid-central	2 parishes
South Central	1 parish
Mid Central	1 parish

Table 5.0
Combined Samples Demographics

	Parishioners without PLCs	Parishioners with PLCs
Sex (Female)	58.00%	66.00%
Age		
20-30	11	8
30-40	23	28
40-50	21	22
50-60	23	16
61+	24	27
Marital Status		
Single	11	9
Married	67	77
Div/Single	2	4
Div/Married	11	3
Widowed	9	8
# of Children		
0	17	15
1	6	10
2 to 3	46	44
4 to 5	20	20
6+	11	11
Yrs of Marriage		
0 to 5	3	5
6 to 10	7	9
11 to 15	13	16
16 to 20	17	15
20+	60	55
Member of Parish Comm. (Yes)	71	71
Education (Self)		
8 Yrs. or Less	13	6
Some H.S.	7	4
H.S.	33	34
Some College	20	18
Technical	7	12
College	8	13
Some Graduate	3	8
Graduate	9	5

	Parishioners without PLCs	Parishioners with PLCs
Education (Spouse)		
8 Yrs. or Less	**10**	9
Some H.S.	**8**	7
H.S.	**34**	34
Some College	**24**	17
Technical	13	**15**
College	6	**9**
Some Graduate	2	**5**
Graduate	3	**5**
Kind of Education		
Catholic Grade	32	**41**
Catholic Jr. High	24	**32**
Catholic High	26	26
Catholic College	**20**	19
Occupation (Self)		
Unskilled	16	**17**
Semiskilled	**17**	11
Skilled	24	**26**
Clerical	32	**35**
Professional	11	11
Occupation (Spouse)		
Unskilled	**18**	13
Semiskilled	**20**	15
Skilled	25	**31**
Clerical	28	28
Professional	9	**13**

A total of 281 questionnaires were mailed to parishioners in these six parishes, questionnaires that were similar to the ones mailed to parishioners who have PLCs. We received 183 useable questionnaires in return, or 65 percent of the original sample. The following data and generalizations come from these parishioners. It is problematic to apply these generalizations to other parishes since the parishes were chosen according to personal judgment by a small number of bishops and pastors.

Demographic Profile—The parishioners without PLCs who answered the study's questionnaire are overrepresented among married females and underrepresented in comparison to the parishioners with PLCs. They are somewhat underrepresented in the 20-to-30-year age category from the PLC parishioners, they have been married fewer years, are more single and more divorced and are from a somewhat lower social class than parishioners in the PLC sample. There are more married men and single women than in the PLC parishioner sample.

B. Who Is Qualified to Pastor the Parish

1. Criteria

Parishioners were asked who, among a list of possible candidates, would they say is qualified to "pastor" their parish in the event they would lose a full-time resident priest. Their choices are compiled below:

Table 5.1
Who is Qualified to Pastor the Parish
(1) Part-time priest   91%
(2) Deacon   82
(3) Religious   79
(4) Married man   46
(5) Married woman   42
(6) Married couple   40

Parishioners were instructed to choose as many from the list as they felt were qualified. These parishioners carved a sharp dichotomy between traditional Church leaders—part-time priest, deacon and religious—and the nontraditional leader—lay man, lay woman and married couple. Clearly these parishioners make a distinction between candidates in the first category and those in the second, based most likely upon the ordination of the priest and deacon and the superior training and background of the sister or brother. While preferring the former category, it is interesting to note that four to five out of ten of these parishioners did not rule out "ordinary" lay persons for "pastoring" in their parishes. From here on we will refer to these pastor candidates as priests (meaning part-time priests) and nonpriests (the deacon, religious, lay man, lay woman, and married couple).

When asked what criteria would qualify a person to pastor their parish, parishioners replied thus:

Table 5.2
Qualifications to Pastor My Parish

(1) Religious education
(2) Status of a deacon or higher
(3) Appropriate training
(4) Loving/caring attitude toward parishioners
(5) Dedication
(6) Understanding needs of people
(7) None other than ordination

When asked what would disqualify one of these persons from "pastoring" their parish, the top responses were:

Table 5.3
Factors Disqualifying Persons from Pastoring My Parish

(1) Lack of knowledge
(2) Lack of training
(3) Lack of dedication
(4) Inability to say Mass
(5) Lack of ordination

---

2. Diocesan Plans for Parishes with Nonresident Priests

Parishioners were asked if they knew of any diocesan-level plan to remove the resident priest in their parish within the next five years. It should be remembered that each of these parishes had actually been suggested by their bishops as liable for a future PLC. Only about one third (36 percent) of these parishioners said that they were aware of such a plan. This awareness, however, coupled with their attitude toward who is qualified to pastor their parish make an interesting correlation. When parishioners say they are aware of such a plan they are also more likely to say a nonpriest would be qualified to pastor in their parish.

3. Specific Plans for Parishes

In addition to a general awareness of a diocesan plan, the parishioners were consulted on their perceptions of specific future plans for their parish. They were asked whether their parish might become pastored by a multiparish priest, a multiparish cluster, a multiparish team or a PLC within the next five years. Their responses were:

Table 5.4 Parishioners' Awareness of Pastoring Plans for Their Parishes	
Multiparish priest	60% (aware of the plan)
Multiparish team	30
Multiparish cluster	47
PLC	29

As with the knowledge of a diocesan plan to move the parish to a part-time priest, parishioners who perceived that their parishes were moving toward either a multiparish priest, team, cluster or PLC mode of pastoring were also more likely to say that all nonpriests mentioned earlier are qualified to pastor their parish. Those that did not feel their parish was moving in one of these directions were less inclined to say these persons are qualified to pastor their parish.

4. How Choice of PLC Should Be Made

Further information was sought on how parishioners felt the choice of a PLC for their parish should be made, if it ever came to that. At least 27 percent felt it would be all right for their parish to make this decision on their own, but 70 percent wanted it made by both the parish and the diocese. Only 2 percent wanted the diocese to decide on this matter by itself. While some will see this as evidence for a certain kind of congregationalism among Catholic parishioners, a stronger case could be made from these data for shared decision-making as revealed in the recent survey by D'Antonio.[1] Data in this study revealed that

---

1. D'Antonio, William D., et al. *American Catholic Laity in a Changing Church* (Kansas City: Sheed & Ward, 1989).

Catholics in general want to be consulted by their dioceses. Our data further substantiates this conclusion.

An curious pattern emerges when this item is correlated with the question of who is qualified to pastor the parish. When lay men, women and couples are thought qualified to pastor their parish, parishioners also feel that the parish alone should make the decision of using a PLC. However, when part-time priests, deacons and religious are felt better qualified, parishioners feel that the parish and the diocese together should make the decision. Perhaps it is understood that religious and ordained come under the authority of the bishop, whereas lay persons make decisions for themselves.

Statistically significant evidence exists showing that when parishioners perceive that either their diocese and/or parish are moving toward a change in the traditional pastoring arrangement, they likewise are more inclined to approve of non-priests for "pastoring" roles in their parishes. This may be interpreted as giving support to those dioceses and parishes that want to get out from under the burden created by the priest shortage by using the newly evolving lay pastoral ministers. An official blessing to such change would in effect "inoculate" parishioners to accept other changes that may be coming.

Thus, the "psychology of inevitability" created by Church leaders in this situation may help parishioners resolve the mental reservations they may have had about nonpriest "pastors." While our data show that they far prefer an ordained or even religious person pastoring them (see Hoge, 1988), they still believe that lay persons can fill the bill. And, when given official blessing, these parishioners would appear to "mentally leapfrog" ahead of Catholics in other situations for whom such a pastoring option is unthinkable or at least highly questioned.

5. Demographic Profile

The parishioners who are more inclined to accept non-priests as "pastors" came from the following categories as shown in Table 5.5.

The more tolerant, open parishioners tend to have higher occupational status, a Catholic education, are single or divorced, are younger persons with few or no children, and one who do not belong to a parish community. Those parishioners who may be having a harder time accepting lay men and women into the pastoring role are from a lower occupational class, public school educated, married, older with more children and members of a parish community.

Table 5.5
Demographic Profile
of Parishioners Accepting Nonpriest Pastors

(1) High status occupation
(2) High level of education
(3) Catholic education
(4) Single men and women
(5) Male
(6) Divorced
(7) Under 60 years of age
(8) Under 21 years of marriage
(9) Few children
(10) Don't belong to a parish community

C. Parishioner Views on Having a PLC and Part-time Priest

Parishioners were asked not only who would be qualified to pastor in their parish if a full-time priest was not available, but specifically how they would feel if they had a PLC doing the "pastoring" with a part-time priest. Parishioners were asked to mark their feelings along a continuum from one extreme emotion to another. They were given pairs of adjectives such as "happy-sad," "cold-warm," "satisfied-dissatisfied," "angry-glad," and "frustrated-contented." Percentages summarizing the positive, moderate and negative points of these responses are presented below. It can be seen that parishioners have negative emotions of sadness and dissatisfaction over this decision to bring a PLC to the parish but are somewhat less inclined to be outright frustrated, cold or angry.

1. Diocesan Plan

We went on to explore the connections between parishioner emotions and the questions about diocesan and parish plans for the future as we did in the area of pastor candidates. We found several parallels. When parishioners feel that their diocese has a plan to move toward a part-time, nonresident priest, they also feel more positive all around about the eventuality of a part-time priest/PLC arrangement for their parish. These relationships are statistically very significant. Perceiving that their dioceses are prepared to move to nontraditional pastoring is associated with positive emotions about having a PLC.

Table 5.6 Feelings if PLC Came to My Parish			
	Negative	Moderate	Positive
(1) Happy/sad	62 %	27 %	11 %
(2) Satisfied/dissatisfied	46	36	18
(3) Frustrated/contented	32	37	32
(4) Cold/warm	27	51	22
(5) Angry/glad	22	53	25

2. Type of Plan for Part-time Priest

As before, when parishioners perceive that their parish may adopt a multiparish priest, cluster, team or PLC arrangement, they also feel more positively about having a PLC in their own parish. Parishioners apparently come to view the PLC positively as an inevitable course for the future when diocesan or parish "imprimaturs" are perceived to exist. While parishioners would prefer to keep the priest-pastor arrangement of the past, they can quickly change when they see such change approved by those higher up in their Church. In those dioceses where this arrangement is not given official sanction, one can only speculate what parishioners are perceiving.

Some important questions arise here concerning the influence of leadership. Do parishioners approve of and accept PLCs after the diocese makes the plans and promulgates them? Do they disapprove of and reject PLCs when the diocese resists planning and casts an official doubt? The role of leadership may be paramount to success in transition dioceses. Perhaps Catholics in their parishes are simply looking for some official recognition that the PLC is a viable and accepted option for parishes moving closer to becoming priestless. Data presented later will show that parishioners give abundant approval for PLC-like roles for the laity. Strong diocesan/parish leadership may be an influencing factor.

3. Demographic Profile

The following shows the categories of parishioners who are most likely to react positively to the possibility of their parish having a PLC in the future.

D. Parishioner Approval of Eight Lay Roles

In a series of questions, parishioners were asked to imagine their parishes in the future. Under one scenario they would have a full-time, resident priest-pastor as they now do. Under a second scenario they would have only a part-time, nonresident priest-pastor. They were then asked to say which of eight ministerial roles—the same ones discussed in the preceding chapter—they think would be appropriate for a lay person to perform under each of those scenarios. Under the first scenario we can get some idea of the extent to which they feel lay persons should be involved in their parishes. Under the second scenario, we could test to see if they would be more tolerant of newer roles if there were no resident priest.

The eight roles, as we have described, include many that are normally relegated to a priest, and all resemble the job description of the parish life coordinator: (1) parish life coordination, (2) planning liturgies, (3) giving homilies, (4) counseling parishioners, (5) visiting the sick and elderly, (6) conducting certain services, (7) presiding over Communion services and (8) preparing parishioners for the sacraments. Again, we wanted to know if parishioners would find it acceptable for other lay persons like themselves to do what the PLC does. Furthermore, we wanted to know if their acceptance of these

---

Table 5.7
Demographic Profile
of Parishioners Who Are Positive About PLC

(1) Catholic college education
(2) Married men
(3) Single women
(4) Never married, divorced and remarried,
      widowed
(5) Male
(6) Married more than 21 years
(7) 51 years of age or older
(8) Don't belong to parish community

---

roles increased when faced with becoming a nonresident priest parish.

After parishioners were asked to comment on the appropriateness of these roles for lay persons, they were then asked if they personally would be interested in doing any of these roles if they were properly trained. Finally, they were asked to comment on their own willingness to be trained for these roles. Thus we measured these eight roles three different ways: (1) their appropriateness for lay people in general, (2) the level of interest in these roles by the specific parishioner being questioned and (3) the willingness to be trained for one or several of these roles.

When these data were analyzed, high levels of appropriateness, interest, and willingness to be trained emerged, as found in the table below. For all eight roles, parishioners in general were willing to admit that these actions are more appropriate for lay persons when there is not a resident priest in the parish. Still, high levels of appropriateness appear for all roles even when the parish has a full-time resident priest. Percentages of acceptance ranged from 92 percent to 43 percent under the first scenario (a full-time priest in the parish). Percentage of acceptance for the second scenario (part-time priest) ranged from 93 to 47 percent.

It can be seen from the table that activities judged more appropriate, the ones at the top of the list, are closer to traditional lay roles. Those judged less appropriate, toward the

Table 5.8
Rank of Roles for the Laity
From Most Appropriate to Least Appropriate

Scenario I (Full-time Priest)	Scenario II (Part-time Priest)
(1) Visit sick (92%)	(1) Visit sick (93%)
(2) Conduct services (75%)	(2) Conduct services (80%)
(3) Sacramental prep. (68%)	(3) Parish life coord. (73%)
(4) Plan liturgies (63%)	(4) Plan liturgies (67%)
(5) Parish life coord. (62%)	(5) Sacramental prep. (66%)
(6) Communion services (51%)	(6) Communion services (59%)
(7) Give homilies (47%)	(7) Give homilies (52%)
(8) Counsel (43%)	(8) Counsel (47%)

bottom of the list, are more traditionally priest roles. It will further be noted that most of the eight roles are ranked in the same order in both scenarios (planning liturgies and parish life coordination are the only ones that change rank), indicating that the presence or absence of a priest does not change their relative acceptability or unacceptability. Parish life coordination receives a full 11 percent change from Scenario I to Scenario II, the greatest degree of change in the favorable direction for any of the eight roles. The PLC role becomes the third most acceptable thing for lay persons to do if they do not have a resident priest.

E. Factors Involved in Approval of Eight Roles

1. Emotional Reaction to Future PLC/Part-time Priest

It is important to understand what factors are related to the approval of some of the eight roles and the disapproval of others. For example, one might speculate that if a parishioner had a positive emotional response to the prospect of a PLC coming to their parish, they might also be inclined to find these nontraditional roles for laity to be appropriate. Because one nontraditional role (PLC) is seen as appropriate for a lay person, many other nontraditional roles may also. The data support this notion under both scenarios, although it is stronger under the second scenario where life without a resident priest is imagined.

2. Future of the Parish Five Years from Now

If parishioners believe that their parish may be without a priest within the next five years (or even at a later date), it would be argued that they would think that more nontraditional lay roles are needed to take up the slack. The data support this argument in that those who believe that they may lose their resident priest within the next five years are more likely to find the eight roles to be appropriate. Additionally, those who feel that their parish may move in this direction even later should also be more inclined to accept these new roles, and this also is supported by the data. Fully 20 percent believe they will be without a priest in the next five years and another 47 percent think this may happen in the more distant future. The other 33 do not believe their parish will ever be without a priest—even though all these parishes were specifically selected by their bishops as possible candidates to lose their resident priests.

3. Diocesan Planning Toward Nonresident Priests

If our earlier argument is true concerning the role of dioceses in leading their parishioners to accept newer forms of parish pastoring, then one would also expect parishioners who perceive that the diocese is planning to remove their resident priest would accept more readily the nontraditional roles for laity. Our data bear out this supposition.

This pattern also holds when parishioners perceive that the diocese is making arrangements for parish clustering, teams and PLCs. All of these relationships are more significant under the second scenario, in which parishioners imagine that their parish will have a nonresident priest.

So we have found strong evidence that parishioners find the nontraditional roles for laity appropriate (1) when they feel positively about the prospect of a PLC in their parish in the future, (2) when they perceive that their parish will be without a resident priest in the future and (3) when they believe their diocese has a plan for parishes without a resident priest.

4. Demographic Profile

The following is a demographic profile of the parishioners who are most accepting of the eight new roles for the laity.

Table 5.9
Demographic Profile
of Parishioners Approving Eight Lay Roles

(1) High Status occupation
(2) Catholic education
(3) Single and married women
(4) Single
(5) Divorced and remarried
(6) Females
(7) Fewer years of marriage
(8) Middle-aged
(9) Few to many children
(10) Not a member of a parish community

F. Personal Interest in Eight Roles for Laity

1. Diocesan Planning Toward Nonresident Priest

The hope would be that if dioceses are going to have to plan for some parishes to be without full-time resident priests, then parishioners would be willing to take up some of the slack after the pastor leaves, retires or dies. Our data support this notion in so far as parishioners who say that they think that their diocese has a plan to move their parish to a PLC arrangement are more inclined to say that they are personally interested in performing the eight nontraditional roles for the laity. Likewise, when these parishioners said that they were aware of plans for a multiparish priest, cluster, team or PLC for their parish they were most likely to be personally interested in the roles.

As in other findings presented in this study, we see the importance of parishioners being informed of diocesan or parish pastoral plans for the future. Furthermore, when parishioners felt that both their parish and the diocese should collaborate in deciding on a PLC for their parish they also were most inclined to be interested in the roles. Knowing about a plan seems to be coupled with a positive outlook on the future of the parish. Perhaps the existence of a plan gives parishioners a sense of security and leads to an accepting mood.

The table below ranks personal *interest* in the eight roles.

Table 5.10
Personal Interest in Eight Lay Roles

(1) Visit sick (55%)
(2) Conduct services (34%)
(3) Communion services (29%)
(4) Sacramental preparation (28%)
(5) Counsel (27%)
(6) Plan liturgies (26%)
(7) PLC (18%)
(8) Give homilies (16%)

Comparing this table with the earlier table on parishioner *approval* of the eight roles reveals that judging a role appropriate does not necessarily translate into taking a personal interest in it. Nevertheless, there is a fair amount of interest in visiting the sick and conducting certain services. Being a PLC and giving homilies are the least interesting.

2. Foreseeing the Parish Without a Resident Priest

As if in preparation, parishioners who believe that their parish will not have a priest within five years or more are also the ones most likely to take a personal interest in the eight roles. This would seem to indicate a strong interest among the laity to "carry on" with the work of their priest. This leads us to hope that when the day does come that the parish loses its priest, the laity will actually respond.

3. Emotional Reaction to Prospect of Part-time Priest/PLC

Those whom we reported above as having positive feelings about having a PLC in their parish some day are the ones who also are most inclined to say they are personally interested in performing the eight lay roles. It is not clear which is the cause and which is the effect. It could be that because they are personally interested in these roles they feel positive toward the PLC. Conversely, those who feel negatively about the future prospect of a PLC in their parish are inclined to say they are not interested in the roles.

4. Demographic Profile

Much of the information presented thus far paints a picture of a type of parishioner who is ready to embrace the future head on and to do what he or she can do to make sure that parish life goes on. Below is the demographic profile of the parishioners who are personally interested in performing the eight newer roles for laity. This represents a more serious group than that of parishioners who simply approve of these roles.

Table 5.11
Demographic Profile
of Parishioners Who Are Personally Interested
in the Eight Lay Roles

(1) Higher status occupation
(2) Higher level of education
(3) Catholic education
(4) Single
(5) Under 50 years of age
(6) Few or no Children
(7) Not a member of a parish community

G. Willingness to be Trained for Lay Roles

So far we have shown that in varying degrees parishioners approve of the eight more radical roles for the laity. They feel more strongly when facing the future without a resident priest, but are still accepting even under the traditional condition of a parish with a resident priest. Furthermore, these same parishioners voiced a high degree of personal interest in performing these roles. Finally, we asked these Catholics if they would be willing to be trained for any of these roles. As can be seen from the following table, sizeable percentages said they would be willing to take the training, education and time involved in becoming proficient in these roles. Anywhere between 12 percent and 35 percent of these parishioners reported that they were willing to be trained to become PLCs, homilists, sacramental preparers and leaders of various services within the context of their parishes.

If our findings can be generalized and we had a hypothetical parish of only 100 eligible parishioners who could fill these roles, then the parish would have a pool of from 12 to 35 persons saying they would be willing to train for these nontraditional lay activities. Of course, the numbers who would actually materialize are likely to be much smaller. Nonetheless, a parish hypothetically would have a pool of 12 persons who say they would be willing to be trained to become a parish life coordinator, for example.

It should be kept in mind that many of the eight roles would require only a few eager parishioners—these roles could be adequately filled even in a small parish. It would seem then that these data are extraordinarily encouraging news for Catholics who feel that a trained lay ministry is a major alternative to the unsanctioned married priesthood. The Church may not have figured out how to finance the training and maintenance of lay ministers in a variety of roles similar to that suggested in our research, but our data strongly indicate that there will be no shortage of human resources when these services are needed.

Table 5.12 Parishioners Willing to be Trained for Lay Roles (Parishioners without PLCs)	
(1) Visit sick/elderly	35%
(2) Conduct certain services	28%
(3) Sacramental preparation	26%
(4) Plan liturgies	19%
(5) Counsel parishioners	19%
(6) Conduct Communion services	19%
(7) Give homilies	12%
(8) Parish life coordination	12%

Regarding the relationship between willingness to be trained and the contributing factors we studied, by and large the same patterns appear here as above. Whether the diocese has a plan to move the parish toward a part-time priest, whether the parishioner foresees the parish without a resident priest in the future, and whether the emotional response of the parishioner over the prospect of the part-time priest/PLC arrangement is positive, the same patterns emerged as we saw for the personal interest variable.

The demographic characteristics of the willing parishioners and the interested parishioners are the same in the following categories: high level of education, Catholic education, high occupational status, few or no children, and not a member of a parish community. There were some differences in the following variables: Marital status: the divorced and single show the most interest. Sex: males predominate in willingness to be trained for Communion services, counseling parishioners and giving homilies; females in visiting the sick, conducting certain services, sacramental preparation, planning liturgies and parish life coordination. Age: same as for interest (under 50) but a lesser tendency for those in their 40s to want to be trained than those in their 50s. Years of marriage: those married 11 to 15 years and those married 21 years and more are the most interested in being trained. This more than likely reflects the greater age of those married longer.

H. Summary

The following is a summary of the more conclusive findings in our survey of parishioners without PLCs:

- Those parishioners who are the most likely to find non-priests (deacons, sisters, lay men, lay women and married couples) qualified to "pastor" their parish are those who (1) are aware of a diocesan plan to deploy part-time priests in diocesan parishes; (2) are aware of specific plans by the diocese to use multiparish priests, clusters, teams or PLCs; and (3) feel the decision to place a PLC in their parish should be a joint parish-diocesan decision.

- Parishioners who are the most likely to have positive feelings at the prospect of having a PLC in their parish at some time in the future are those who (1) are aware of a diocesan plan to deploy part-time priests in diocesan parishes, and (2) are aware of plans by the diocese to use multiparish priests, clusters, teams or PLCs.

- Parishioners who are most likely to feel that eight nontraditional roles for laity are appropriate, are personally interested in them and are willing to seek training are those who (1) are aware of a diocesan plan to deploy part-time priests in diocesan parishes; (2) are aware of specific plans by the diocese to use multiparish priests, clusters, teams or PLCs; (3) feel the decision to place a PLC in their parish should be a joint parish-diocesan decision; (4) express positive emotions at the prospect of having a PLC in their parish at some time in the future; and (5) believe that their parish will be without a resident priest within the next five years or even later.

6.

Conclusions

The *Institute for Pastoral Life's Study of Parish Life Coordinators* represents the largest empirical study of the phenomenon of parish life coordinators to date. Ours was a study of 102 PLCs, 86 dioceses and 568 parishioners. We used five separate research instruments to measure several facets of PLC work in our sample of parish life coordinators. We further used these instruments to gain a more complete understanding of PLC conditions in dioceses that now have them, and to find out what may motivate other dioceses to adopt the PLC model. Finally, we sought the reactions of parishioners who have been experiencing the PLC as well as the perceptions of parishioners who may have PLCs in coming years. The result is a comprehensive data base that should provide a mass of information for policy makers, practitioners and scholars alike.

Our purpose in this last chapter is to pull together our findings and to make some policy suggestions in each of the study areas. First, we will recap each of the five samples: the PLCs themselves, parishioners with PLCs, parishioners without PLCs, dioceses with PLCs and dioceses without PLCs. Second, we will draw several conclusions based upon all five samples taken together. Finally, we will make an overall conclusion to our study.

A. Parish Life Coordinators

1. Policy

Based on the work found in Chapter 1, "Responses from Parish Life Coordinators," we have looked at the impact of 11 policy components that affect PLCs in four main areas of their ministerial life: affirming relationships, nonaffirming relationships, role ambiguity and their emotional states. The 11 components were diocesan ministries (how the PLC ministry relates to the various ministries of the diocese), parish ministries (how the PLC ministry relates to other ministries in the parish), diocesan plans concerning future need of PLCs, diocese-parish coordination, parish accountability, salary, contracts, benefits, length of contract and internship.

The PLCs were then asked to state how *adequate* or *inadequate* each of the 11 policies were. They ranked the following seven as most inadequate.

Table 6.1
Inadequate Policies According to PLCs

(1) Internship
(2) Coordination
(3) Diocesan ministries
(4) Diocesan plan
(5) Parish ministries
(6) Diocesan accountability
(7) Salary

The table below extends the analysis of the importance of all 11 policies by showing each's statistically significant impact on the four studied areas of the PLC's ministerial life. In other words, how many times did an absent or inadequate policy on diocesan accountability affect role ambiguity? emotions? affirming relationships? nonaffirming relationships?

	Table 6.2				
	Impact of Inadequate Policies on PLC's Ministerial Life				
Policy	Ambiguity	Emotions	Affirming	Nonaffirming	Total
(1) Diocesan accountability	2	2	2	2	8
(2) Diocesan ministries	2	0	2	2	6
(3) Internships	2	1	1	1	5
(4) Diocese-parish coordination	1	1	2	1	5
(5) Parish ministries	2	0	0	2	4
(6) Benefits	1	1	1	1	4
(7) Contract length	1	1	1	1	4
(8) Salary	1	0	2	0	3
(9) Contracts	1	1	1	0	3
(10) Diocesan Plan	0	2	1	0	3
(11) Parish accountability	0	1	0	1	2

By referring to the table we can see that an absent or inadequate diocesan accountability policy has an impact twice in each of the four areas for a total of eight significant impacts. By contrast the parish accountability policy ranked last among the 11 policies as it had an impact only twice in the four areas.

Based on this way of measuring the impact of PLC policy, the following were the seven most influential policies.

Table 6.3
Policies Most Influential on Ministerial Life
(1) Diocesan accountability
(2) Diocesan ministries
(3) Internships
(4) Diocese-parish coordination
(5) Parish ministries
(6) Benefits
(7) Contract length

By comparing the policies that the PLCs most often said were inadequate (above) and the policies found most influential on ministerial life here we find five in common which enables us to narrow the list down to five most influential policies.

Table 6.4
Policies Most Influential to the PLC

(1) Internship
(2) Coordination of diocesan and parish PLC plans
(3) Diocesan ministries
(4) Parish ministries
(5) Diocesan accountability

We will comment on the policy implications of these finding at the end of this section. For now we will conclude by saying that these five policies seem to be the most important in that their absence or inadequacy have the most negative impact on PLC life.

2. Planning

Diocesan planning—We asked PLCs if they felt any ambiguity about their PLC role because of inadequate diocesan planning. Each PLC was free to interpret diocesan planning as she or he understood that term to mean. Five conclusions can be reached from the data presented on diocesan planning found in Chapter II on parish life coordinators. When the PLC perceives diocesan *planning to be inadequate*, she also: (1) believes that many of the 11 policy areas are absent, (2) perceives her role in reference to diocesan expectations to be ambiguous, (3) perceives her role in reference to parish expectations to be less ambiguous, (4) believes certain elements of her role are not working properly, (5) has no particular emotional reaction to the inadequacy.

The implications of these findings are that if PLCs perceived that the dioceses were up to par with planning, then PLCs would also perceive that PLC policies do exist in the 11 policy areas, role ambiguity would lessen with respect to diocesan expectations but increase with the parish (because of conflicting expectations) and the PLC would perceive that her work in general is going well. The fact that better diocesan planning would exacerbate the PLC's sense of role ambiguity regarding parishioner expectations suggests that more *careful joint planning* is needed between the diocese and the parish and its parishioners.

Parish planning—The PLCs were also asked if they felt any ambiguity in their role stemming from inadequate parish planning as they defined it. From Chapter 2 the following conclusions about PLCs' perceptions of parish planning can be reached. If the PLC sees this planning to be inadequate she also: (1) still sees many of the 11 policy areas as adequate, (2) feels her job is not going completely well, (3) nevertheless does not experience role ambiguity with her parish, (4) has negative emotional reactions to the inadequacies.

The implications are that if parishes do a better job of planning then they can expect their PLCs to see many of the 11 policies as inadequate, to have a better sense of job satisfaction, experience more parish role ambiguity (because of conflicting expectations) and experience more positive emotions.

Again we are caught in an incongruity between levels of planning. If diocesan planning is seen as adequate, the PLC will experience less role ambiguity from the diocese; but if parish planning is seen as adequate, the PLC will experience more role ambiguity from the parish. At the same time she will say that the 11 PLC policies (largely set at the diocesan level) are inadequate. If the PLC believes that parish planning is inadequate she not only will experience role ambiguity with the parish but also negative emotions—feeling burned out, unsupported, not needed, etc. One can conclude that the PLC is placed under contradictory expectations and is actually *experiencing role conflict, not just role ambiguity.*

PLC planning—Finally PLCs were asked if they thought their own planning, or formation, for the PLC role was adequate or inadequate. When PLC formation is perceived to be inadequate, as admitted by the PLC, the following correlates appear: (1) she believes that the 11 PLC policies are either present or adequate, (2) she experiences negative emotions, (3) she does not experience diocesan role ambiguity, (4) but she does experience parish role ambiguity.

This implies that with better formation the PLC will look at the policy areas more critically, judging them as either absent or inadequate. She will see an improvement in her emotional state, but while there will be less parish-induced role ambiguity she will feel more ambiguity in reference to the diocese—perhaps because of her more critical view of PLC policies. Once again, lack of planning creates inconsistencies in the PLC's status. It is evident that not all ambiguity can be planned away. The better formed the PLC, the more inadequate she will find the policies and the greater tension will exist between diocesan and parish expectations.

3. Role Ambiguity

Diocesan sources—Role ambiguity exists when the diocese places unclear expectations on the PLC or when her work does not match diocesan expectations. The following were found to be related to greater amounts of role ambiguity coming from the diocese: (1) negative nonaffirming relations between the PLC and the canonical pastor and sacramental minister; (2) negative affirming relations (referring to a sociological type) between the PLC and the canonical pastor and the sacramental minister; (3) negative relations between the PLC and personnel in the parish, deanery and diocese; (4) perceptions by the PLC that the 11 PLC policies are absent or inadequate; (5) negative emotional states.

Parish sources—The following general conclusions were reached concerning higher levels of role ambiguity stemming from the parish: (1) negative nonaffirming relations between the PLC and the sacramental minister; (2) negative affirming relations between the PLC and the canonical pastor; (3) negative relations between the PLC and personnel from the parish, deanery and diocese; (4) negative emotional states.

Policy suggestions—From our study, then, the following related suggestions would lead to less role ambiguity and improved PLC performance and job satisfaction.

(1) Dioceses should institutionalize adequate policies with respect to PLCs. In particular, among the 11 policy areas we studied, policies dealing with internships for PLCs, coordination of diocesan and parish plans concerning PLCs,

the role of the PLC in the context of all diocesan and parish ministries, and the place of the PLC in diocesan accountability.

(2) Institutionalized PLC policies should foster more positive relations between the PLC and the canonical pastor, sacramental minister, and other parish, deanery and diocesan personnel.

(3) Improved relations in these areas could reduce role ambiguity.

(4) Lessened role ambiguity should lead to more positive emotional states in the PLC.

4. PLC Needs

The PLCs mentioned several areas of job satisfaction, or fulfilled needs, which can be placed under two categories: (1) *making it possible for a faith community to exist* (sharing the lives of people in a public ministry, enabling people, recognizing God in people's lives, forming and leading communities) and (2) *personal fulfillment* (being needed, staying active and challenged, personal spirituality).

Unfulfilled needs fall into several categories, the one most frequently mentioned being *poor relations* (lack of diocesan support, being treated as an unequal, poor relations with the priests and lack of collaboration). It has already been suggested that if the 11 PLC policies we studied were institutionalized, these relations might improve.

The other main category of unfulfilled needs stems from the *parish location*. Feelings of isolation, lack of resources, being unchallenged and lack of professional counseling suggest difficulties related to a small, rural parish. Dioceses and deaneries will need to offer whatever support they can to overcome these difficulties.

5. Formation of the PLC

Data presented in Chapter 2 show that advanced degrees and educational experience top the list of a PLC's formal formation. Informal formation includes various parish and diocesan assignments, such as parish ministry, teaching and administration, plus personal experience.

We received one unexpected answer to our question concerning what was required to be a PLC in the parish. The most frequent answer was that there were no formal requirements at all. This suggests that PLCs sometimes get appointed in a happenstance manner. It also points to the rather nebulous nature of parish life coordination as it exists in some dioceses. In the less frequent instances in which requirements are stated they involve three things: advance degrees, experience and an application process.

PLCs have found their formation adequate for the job in that their backgrounds have provided the requisite experience, knowledge, skill and awareness in order to "pastor" a parish. It is revealing, however, that when asked what has been most inadequate about their formation experience, PLCs answered most frequently that they had no formal preparation. This again calls attention to the unofficial manner in which some PLCs are appointed to "pastor" their parishes. This is reinforced by the next two most frequent answers: PLCs say they are lacking in experience and are doing a job for which they are not trained. Beyond these, PLCs tend to cite only inadequacies in specific professional skills (such as finance, marriage and family law, sacraments, organizing, counseling, homiletics, Canon Law and knowledge of rural culture.)

Policy suggestions—These inadequacies suggest the following policy actions:

(1) Structure appointments to parishes so that PLC candidates are adequately prepared and experienced through internships, parish/diocesan experience and a clear job description.

(2) Establish adequate formation courses, workshops and degree curricula to include instruction in parish finance, Canon Law (particularly with respect to marriage and family), the sacraments, homiletics, rural culture and group dynamics.

(3) Clarify diocesan policies on how PLC work fits into the broader array of diocesan policies and clarify how dioce-

san PLC plans are to be coordinated with parish PLC plans.

6. PLC Evaluation of Their Work

Positive results—PLCs are proud that they are instrumental in helping parishes stay open, that they help keep the faith alive among Catholics who might otherwise not have such a community, that they are accepted by their parishioners, that they have good relationships with their priests, that people are being enabled and served and that the PLCs themselves have adequate authority to carry out their job.

Since these are stated as positive outcomes there is no need to make policy suggestions concerning them. We might add that these responses are echoed by the parishioners with PLCs. When asked what were the rewards of having a PLC they most often answered that the PLC keeps things running around the parish, the parish has a person to contact in times of need and problems are being addressed.

Trouble spots—PLCs note several areas of parish life in which they experience some difficulty. (1) Lack of authority: It is interesting to note that while this is the most frequently mentioned area many PLCs feel is not working, it was also mentioned by other PLCs as one of the main areas that was working smoothly. (2) Lack of time: This may be particularly true of PLCs who are married and have families. (3) Cultural clashes: This may come about when a PLC is mismatched with a small, rural or inner-city parish for which she is unprepared. Some of this stems from the PLC's chance "falling into" the job or the parish's or diocese's lack of adequate formation requirements. (4) Poor relationships: Among the top things PLCs mention as not working are poor relationships with the diocese and lack of support by priests, the sacramental minister in particular.

Policy suggestions—A number of things can be done to alleviate some of these trouble spots.

(1) To heighten the authority of the PLC in her parish, policies that clearly show how the PLC ministry fits in with the other ministries of both the diocese and the parish will give parishioners a greater sense that this is something the

Church strongly sponsors. Other practices that would reinforce the authority of the PLC are a clear-cut policy on the role of PLCs in the diocese—which would also serve to improve PLC/sacramental minister/canonical pastor relationships—clear lines of diocesan accountability, an internship in the parish before appointment and the presence of the bishop or his delegate at an installation ceremony. The diocese and the priests need to do everything they can to convey to the parishioner that this person is doing an essential task that is sanctioned by the "official" Church.

(2) Concerning lack of time, the Church needs to help in any way that it can to make time management training available to the PLC. Those PLCs with inadequate training may need to take management and public relations training to help them successfully delegate various ministries for which they are responsible. The PLC role at its best is an exhausting, never-ending job. PLC's need to develop realistic expectations of what is possible for them to do.

(3) Internships and formal courses and workshops on rural culture may be helpful in cultural clashes. Some of these clashes may result from a difference in education between the PLC and the parishioners. Better interpersonal skills and sensitivity to educational differences on her part may be needed.

(4) In the section above on role ambiguity we noted that negative relations between the PLC and priests most often take place when there is little monitoring to check confusion between the PLC's and the priest's role, when there is disagreement over the issue of preaching, when the PLC is not allowed to take an active leadership role in the parish, and when the dissenting parties do not submit their difficulties in the relationship to prayer. It is self-evident that reversing these conditions would help to improve relations. We also noted that more adequate policies dealing with internships, coordination of diocesan and parish PLC plans, diocesan and parish ministries policies and diocesan accountability policies would help bring about better

relations between the PLC and the canonical pastor and sacramental minister.

B. Parishioners With PLCs

The sample of parishioners with PLCs were asked questions about (1) who is qualified to pastor their parish, (2) what roles they feel are appropriate for lay persons and (3) how they evaluate their PLC. We will draw together all of the conclusions we have reached earlier in this book and finish with some policy suggestions.

1. Who Is Qualified to Pastor the Parish

Our data revealed that this important attitude of parishioners is strongly influenced by diocesan, parish and parishioner factors.

Diocesan factors—The following factors were found to be associated with positive parishioner attitudes toward nonpriests as "pastors": (1) they were unaware of any diocesan plan for PLCs, (2) they were unaware or thought their parish was not selected by such a plan, (3) they thought that it had taken a month or more to install their PLC in the parish.

Parish factors—Three factors were found to be associated with a positive attitude toward the qualifications of nonpriests as "pastors" of their parish: (1) they know definitely or believe their parish has been without a resident priest at one time, (2) they have had several PLCs in the parish and (3) they perceive that the relationship between the priest and the PLC has been poor.

Parishioner factors—Several parishioner characters were found to be associated with a positive attitude toward the qualifications of nonpriests as "pastors": (1) they have been supportive of their PLC, (2) they were originally open to the idea of a PLC in the parish, (3) they have had a Catholic high school and college education, (4) they are married women or single men, (5) they are divorced and remarried or widowed, (6) they are young and (7) they are not members of their parish community.

Thus a picture of the parishioner who is most likely to be tolerant of nonpriest pastors emerges: (1) those belonging to certain demographic groups and (2) those who have had an experience of a parish directed by nonpriests.

2. Appropriate Lay Roles, Interest and Training

Our study tried to go beyond simply finding out who the parishioner felt was qualified to pastor their parish. We wanted to know (1) if they thought certain nontraditional ministerial activities similar to those done by a PLC were appropriate for lay persons in general, (2) if they themselves were interested in such roles and (3) if they would seek training for such roles if training were available. We tested these three dimensions on a number of parish and parishioner factors to find predictors of the person most likely to volunteer for tasks similar to those performed by their PLC. As reported earlier in this book we found high levels of support for these roles as well as high levels of interest in training for the roles. The following parish and parishioner factors were found to be associated with high levels of appropriateness, interest and willingness to be trained.

Parish factors—(1) having been without a resident priest in the past, (2) having experienced several PLCs in the parish.

Parishioner factors—(1) feeling that both traditional and nontraditional candidates are qualified to pastor their parish, (2) an openness toward the PLC in the parish, (3) evaluating that the PLC has done the more "priestly" activities well or evaluating that the PLC has not done the more "lay" activities well, (4) falling within certain demographic categories such as married, female, middle aged, single, divorced and now single, and those inactive in the parish community.

Policy suggestions—The above conclusions lead us to suggest that those most likely to be interested in training for PLC-like roles in their parishes are:

(1) Those that have experienced someone other than a priest acting as "pastor" of their parish.

(2) Those with an open attitude toward a PLC and those that feel nontraditional candidates can assume a "pastoring" role in the parish.

(3) Those that have found that the PLC can perform traditional "priestly" roles well.

3. Evaluation of the PLC

The data seem to show a very high level of acceptance of the PLC by the parishioners. For example, when asked how supportive they have been of their PLC, fully 96 percent said they are very supportive or supportive with 54 percent saying they are very supportive. When parishioners evaluated specific aspects of the PLC's performance, they gave very high marks, as follows:

Table 6.5
Parishioner Evaluation the PLC
(4 = Good, 5 = Very good)

(1) Community-building	4.15
(2) Leadership	4.18
(3) Educational work	4.29
(4) Administration	4.30
(5) Crisis ministry	4.30
(6) Diocesan Ministry	4.40
(7) Liturgy	4.44

On none of the indicators did the parishioners give their PLCs more than 20 percent negative ratings. These are high marks indeed. When asked to describe the relations between the PLC and a parish team, if such a team existed, 90 percent said they were very good or good. While 73 percent of the parishioners said they were open or very open to their PLC when he or she first came, 90 percent of them now say they are open or very open to their PLC. Finally, 90 percent of the parishioners say that the relations between their PLC and the priest are good or very good.

The following diocesan, parish and parishioner factors were found to be associated with a *negative evaluation of the PLC.*

Diocesan factors—(1) those who perceive that their parish was not selected by a diocesan PLC plan, (2) those who believe that it was less than one month before their PLC was appointed, (3) those who feel that the diocese had not prepared them well for their PLC.

Parish factors—those who feel that the relations between the PLC and the priest have been poor.

Parishioner factors—(1) those who have been closed to the idea of a PLC in their parish, (2) those who have shown low support for their PLC, (3) those who feel that traditional candidates are better qualified than nontraditional candidates to "pastor" their parishes and (4) those with high school education, male, middle aged, married, single men and the single in general.

Policy suggestions—These generalizations suggest the following steps to take to improve the evaluations of PLCs by their parishioners:

(1) Improve PLC/priest relations by establishing definite PLC policies, especially those involving diocesan accountability of the PLC, how the PLC fits into the diocesan ministries, and diocesan-parish accountability.

(2) Adequately prepare parishioners for the assignment of a PLC.

(3) Give the parish more than a month to prepare for a new PLC.

(4) Encourage parishioners to accept the idea of the PLC as a "pastoral supervisor" of the parish.

(5) Encourage supportive attitudes among parishioners through a "psychology of inevitability" and support.

(6) Make sure PLCs are selected by a diocesan PLC plan of some sort.

C. Parishioners Without PLCs

As with parishioners with PLCs, our primary concerns with parishioners without PLCs were which candidates they felt would be qualified to pastor their parish if no full-time resident priest was available, what nontraditional roles would they deem appropriate for lay persons, and would they themselves be interested in these roles and be willing to seek training.

We found that parishioners were more likely to feel that nontraditional candidates are capable of "pastoring" their parish, to regard nontraditional roles for laity as appropriate, to become personally interested in these nontraditional roles and to be willing to be trained for these roles when the following factors were present: (1) when parishioners were aware that the diocese has a plan for parishes without resident priests, such as multiparish priests, clusters, etc., (2) when parishioners say they have been without a resident priest in their parish, (3) when parishioners have a more positive attitude toward the prospect of a PLC/part-time priest arrangement in their parish and (4) when they fall within the following demographic categories: high occupational status, advanced education, Catholic education, divorced and remarried, single, few or no children and not a member of a parish community.

Policy suggestions—These findings point out that if we want parishioners to be open and accepting of nontraditional "pastors" in their parishes, and if we want to produce parishioners who are themselves willing to subsume these nontraditional roles then we can do the following:

(1) Have a diocesan plan that creates a positive attitude toward the PLC. The consciousness on the part of parishioners that their diocese has a plan to take care of parishes that do not have a resident priest seems to help them accept a PLC in their own parish. It likewise helps them to accept ordinary lay persons doing works traditionally relegated to the ordained. These data would suggest that dioceses want to have such a plan and to promulgate it widely throughout the diocese.

(2) Be aware of parish history. Dioceses and parishes do not have much control over whether their parishioners have had the experience of being in a parish without a resident priest. However, this experience is very powerful in modifying attitudes of parishioners in so far as they are much

more accepting of nonpriests as "pastor" of their parishes and they are more willing to accept and be trained for nontraditional lay roles.

(3) Be aware that those most likely to take a positive attitude toward a PLC/part-time priest in their parish are the young, those with high occupational status, those of advanced and Catholic education, those who are divorced and remarried or single, those with few or no children and those not a member of a parish community.

D. The Dioceses

The following is a summary of the major findings from the sample of 82 dioceses with and without PLCs.

(1) Dioceses with PLCs less often (61 percent) have plans for parishes without resident priests than do the dioceses that presently do not have PLCs (67 percent). Only 15 percent of the PLC dioceses now have such plans and the others say they are just entering the planning stage. This could be of some consequence. The diocesan plan for parishes without resident priests is an influential factor for PLCs. It is related to negative emotional states and some negative relations with the canonical pastor and the sacramental minister. For parishioners, a perception that the diocese does not have such a plan is related to whether they give their PLC a good evaluation or not. Furthermore when parishioners are aware that the diocese has a plan for parishes without resident priests they have a more positive attitude toward the prospect of a PLC/part-time priest in their parish, they are more likely to feel that nonpriests could "pastor" their parish, they think nontraditional roles for laity are appropriate, they are themselves more interested in these nontraditional roles and they are more willing to be trained for these non-traditional roles.

Thus our data reveal that having or not having such a plan in the diocese can have a powerful impact upon both the PLC and the parishioners in those dioceses. Such a plan seems to bring about a number of positive results that should make dioceses want to establish such a plan.

(2) Data from both sets of dioceses would indicate that within the next five years as many as 77 dioceses may be implementing the PLC model to some extent. This projection is based on the presumptions that those dioceses that now use PLCs will continue to do so, those dioceses that say they will adopt this model will in fact do so and at least half of the dioceses that are now uncertain will adopt this practice. Because of the way we sampled dioceses without PLCs (see Chapter 3) it is possible that others not in our study will be moving in this direction.

(3) Dioceses report that there are an assortment of factors encouraging or discouraging the adoption of PLCs.

(4) When four settings were proposed in which the PLC could be used—multiparish priest, team, cluster and a PLC alone in a parish dioceses with PLCs are somewhat more inclined to use the team and the PLC-alone approaches.

(5) Fully one third of dioceses with PLCs are placing them in multiparish priests, clusters and team settings. The remaining two thirds have PLCs serving alone in one or more parishes.

(6) Nearly 40 percent of the dioceses with PLCs said that they have used some PLCs "informally," defined for our study purposes as placing of a PLC without official appointment by the bishop.

(7) Dioceses that deploy the largest number of PLCs are using them mostly in settings in which a priest serves several parishes.

(8) The data show a slowing in the deployment of PLCs in recent years compared with five years ago when PLCs were appointed in a flourish of "pioneering." However, when we asked the dioceses who do not now have PLCs when they intended to deploy PLCs, we get the picture of another boom period in the coming years.

(9) Dioceses that now use PLCs are much more inclined to see the diocese (rather than the parish) as the instigator of the move toward using a PLC in a parish than are the dioceses that are only thinking about the future use of PLCs.

(10) Seven in ten dioceses that use PLCs say that it takes them less than a year between deciding on a PLC and installing one in a parish, with 41 percent saying it takes them from one to six months. When parishioners were asked how long it was before they got their PLC after being notified that they would have a PLC, nearly half of the sample (46 percent) said that it was less than one month. Furthermore, 40 percent of the parishioner sample said that the diocese did not adequately prepare them for the PLC. More extensive analysis of the parishioner data showed that when parishioners believed that they had not been adequately prepared by their diocese and that it was less than one month before their PLC was appointed, parishioners gave more negative evaluations of their PLCs. It would seem that there are more adequate ways dioceses can prepare their parishioners and to be conscious of the time needed to prepare the parish.

(11) Dioceses that use PLCs agree that their PLCs should undergo a formation program that includes one or several of the following: a master's degree in pastoral studies, screening and training of the PLC, and enrollment in a lay pastoral ministry program. These recommendations parallel those of the PLCs themselves, who feel that their formation should include the appropriate master's or bachelor's degree and appropriate experience in parish, school and rural ministry.

(12) Most dioceses with PLCs have lines of accountability to the bishop or the canonical pastor.

(13) While 36 percent of dioceses see the PLC's work as an extension of the priest-pastor of the parish, 98 percent are willing to see it as an extension of both the bishop and the priest-pastor.

(14) The most frequently used advertising methods for PLCs are personal contact, the diocesan newspaper, religious communities, and the present pastoral staff of the diocese.

(15) The most frequent interviewers for the job of PLC are the personnel board and the bishop.

(16) The bishop is the main person who actually does the hiring of the PLC.

(17) While nearly two thirds of the dioceses say that a stated salary, benefits, and contract length are important components of any PLC contract, sizeable minorities (ranging from 37 percent to 56 percent) of the PLCs themselves say that one or more of these contract components are either absent or inadequate. This indicates that components of a PLC contract are a source of consequence to the PLC. Much of the ambiguity and negative feelings that PLCs express stem from contract components. These components have a significant impact not only on role ambiguity and negative emotional states of the PLC but also on the quality of the relations the PLC has with the canonical pastor and sacramental minister.

(18) While about half of the dioceses use some kind of an installation ceremony and many are presided over by the bishop, the local dean, the vicar general or some other diocesan official, one half of the dioceses do not make provision for such public recognition of the ministry. One of the things that the PLCs mention as not working about their role is that they lack the authority they need. Official diocesan recognition by an installation ceremony could have a critical symbolic impact upon both the parishioner and the newly appointed PLC.

(19) Only one in five dioceses make provision for an internship experience for the PLC. In terms of the self admission of the PLC, this was the most inadequate PLC policy of the 11 components studied. Furthermore, in terms of its impact upon PLC role ambiguity, negative emotions, and negative affirming and nonaffirming relations with the canonical pastor and the sacramental minister, the internship was the third most powerful policy in predicting negative states for the PLC.

It is realized that a year-long internship in the parish in which the PLC is to serve may not always be feasible or desirable, but the ideal of a year's experience in the parish would seem to be desirous nonetheless. This kind of experience would allow the future PLC to get to know the history and culture of the parish, to become acquainted with the parishioners, perhaps to work on any role clarification that is needed, to practice "pastoring" under the tutelage of the resident priest, and finally to begin to relate to the deanery and diocesan officials.

(20) Our diocesan data reveal a number of ways that PLCs affiliate with their dioceses. Unfortunately we did not seek any qualitative data from the dioceses on the nature of these relations. When the PLCs were asked to comment on the quality of their relations with parish, deanery and diocesan officials, they told us that while relations with the diocese were the most positive when they first came to the parish, these relations had declined relatively. Because parish relations had improved so dramatically, relations with the diocese were now relatively the lower of the two.

(21) Only 6 percent of the dioceses said that they give financial assistance to their PLCs and fully 60 percent say they give no financial assistance at all. A number of questions about the financing of PLCs in the parish are left unanswered by our study. We have no sense from our study as to whose obligation it is to support the PLC in the parish or whether it is realistic to expect small and often rural parishes to be able to support a PLC on their own. The dioceses do admit this is a problem.

(22) Dioceses find activities of an *outreach* nature (evangelization, help to needy, social justice, crisis intervention) and *proclamation* and *teaching* (teaching religion, RCIA, Bible study, preaching, weddings, wakes) to be the least appropriate activities for a PLC to perform. Activities involving *community life* (visiting the sick and elderly, community building, ecumenical contact) and *administration* (control of finances, conflict management, general parish administration) are judged to be the most appropriate. Perhaps dioceses rank these activities in this way because they view outreach and proclamation and teaching as more in line with a priestly role, whereas community life and administration most closely resemble traditional lay roles.

(23) While 60 percent of dioceses evaluate their PLCs at least once a year, 40 percent of the dioceses do not appear to have a personnel quality control mechanism built in. It is possible that some of the negative dynamics uncovered in PLC relations and some of the negative evaluations given by parishioners are because of poor PLC performance, which could be dealt with more efficiently by an evaluation process of some sort.

(24) Dioceses that have had PLCs in place for some time describe a number of *good results*: relations between the priest and PLC are good, PLCs are effective in this sort of ministry, the diocese has adequately prepared the parishes, parishes are open and functioning, someone is in charge in the parish, the parish has been empowered and the PLC is included in diocesan functioning.

(25) Dioceses that have had PLCs in place for some time mention the following *problems*: parishioners are reluctant to accept this form of ministry, there is insufficient parishioner education on the PLC role, diocesan priests do not accept this form of ministry, the PLC's role is ambiguous and the PLC's formation has been inadequate. While dioceses may feel that there is not enough education of parishioners for the PLC role, it does not translate into a rejection of the PLC by parishioners, as we have seen. Parishioners do, however, hold it against their diocese for not adequately preparing them for the PLC. And, as we have seen, they follow through with lower evaluations of the PLC. We would suggest establishing a formal program to educate the parish on the ministry of the PLC, its connection to the total diocesan pastoral ministry, and role clarification between the PLC, canonical pastor and the sacramental minister.

Our study did not address the rejection of PLCs by the diocesan priests. We can only suggest that the diocese study the options that it has. If the PLC model seems either the only one or one of several options open to the diocese, then the diocese must make clear the benefits and limitations of each approach. Our study shows the many positive results that can come when dioceses have a PLC

Plan and promulgate it fully. The problems and possible solutions to role ambiguity and insufficient formation were discussed above.

E. What's Working, What's Not

The following is a final look at our research, an overview of what we know to date about the PLC model with its strengths and weaknesses. For convenience, we will list what seems to be working with the PLC model and what are the areas of remaining challenge from the viewpoint of each of our samples: the parish life coordinators, dioceses with and without PLCs and parishioners with and without PLCs. It is hoped that this will leave the reader with concrete information from which to consider the PLC model in one's own diocese or parish.

1. What Is Working According to Parish Life Coordinators

• Parish life coordinators list the following positive results of their PLC role in their parishes: they have received parish acceptance, parishioners have been enabled, people have been served, they have adequate authority and there have been good relations in the parish.

• In terms of diocesan/parish policies dealing with PLCs, they have found the contract, salary and benefit components to these policies to be more adequate than those parts dealing with diocesan and parish PLC plans and their coordination.

• Overall, PLCs express only moderate levels of role ambiguity.

• PLCs express a number of positive emotions connected with their role of PLC: they feel well received, as insiders, needed, like staying on, hopeful and successful.

• The following affirming relations between the PLC and the canonical pastor and sacramental minister are expressed: he trusts me in my pastoring role and he shows flexibility toward me in our joint ministry to the parish.

• The following nonaffirming (as a sociological type) relations are expressed as positive between the PLC and the canonical pastor and the sacramental minister: he treats me competently.

• While starting at a high point, there has been significant improvement in the relations between the PLC and the parish, staff and the parish council.

• PLCs express the following personal needs that are being fulfilled by their PLC work in the parish: they are needed, they are sharing their lives with people, they are in public ministry, they are helping to enable people, they are staying active and challenged, they are recognizing God in people's lives, they have a personal spirituality, they are forming faith communities and they are exerting leadership in these communities.

• PLCs feel that their formation for the PLC role has been adequate in the following ways: it has provided experience, given them the necessary knowledge, equipped them with administrative skills, given them appropriate training and made them aware of parish life.

2. Areas of Challenge According to the PLC

• Certain PLC policies need to be institutionalized or improved: internship policies, coordination of parish and diocesan PLC policies, statements on how PLC work fits into the larger ministries of the parish and diocese and how the PLC is accountable to the diocese.

• More adequate diocesan planning (as defined by the PLC) is needed.

• More adequate parish planning (as defined by the PLC) is needed

• PLCs are experiencing role ambiguity with their parishes and dioceses. When there is diocesan ambiguity there is less parish ambiguity. When there is parish ambiguity there is less ambiguity coming from the diocese. PLCs often find themselves caught between their diocese and their parish.

• PLCs express a number of negative emotional states: they feel frustrated, exhausted, inadequately prepared, feel unaccomplished, not regarded as a pastor and unsupported by their priests and bishop.

• In terms of affirming relations with their canonical pastors and sacramental ministers, PLCs feel that the following types of negative relations exist: the priests are not monitoring their relationship with the PLC for possible role confusion, they do not encourage the PLCs to preach, the priests do not repeatedly instruct the parish about the new leadership structure in the parish and they do not submit problems in their joint ministry to prayer.

• In terms of nonaffirming relations with their canonical pastors and sacramental ministers, PLCs feel that there exist uncomfortable feelings, disagreements and confrontations.

• The relations between the PLC and deanery, diocesan officials and the bishop are less positive than between the PLC and the parish.

• PLCs say that with respect to their role they lack authority, they lack sufficient time, there are cultural clashes and there are poor relationships between the PLCs and the sacramental ministers and other priests.

• PLCs express the following problems in their personal needs: they lack diocesan support, there is isolation in their position, they lack resources, they are treated as unequal, there are poor relations with the priests, there is a lack of collaboration, they are not being challenged, they lack professional counseling, there is insufficient time to do their jobs.

• PLCs find the following to be inadequate about their formation experiences: many have had no formal preparation, they lack knowledge of financial affairs of the parish, they lack experience, they are doing a job for which they are not trained, they do not know marriage and family law, they have inadequate knowledge of the sacraments.

3. What Is Working According to the Dioceses

• Our data indicates that as many as 77 dioceses may be using the PLC model within the next five years. A further consolidation of this model should take place.

• To meet the needs of parishes in their dioceses, as many as 40 percent of the dioceses say they have used PLCs in an informal way (without official appointment by the bishop).

• Dioceses seem to be using PLCs primarily to extend the priest's role in settings where one priest serves many parishes. The PLC carries on when the priest is not there.

• The dioceses that say they might use PLCs in the future are more inclined to let the parish instigate the movement to a PLC than are dioceses that presently have PLCs.

• Dioceses and PLCs are in rough agreement on what formation experiences are necessary for doing PLC work.

• Most dioceses (60 percent) make provision for the evaluation of their PLCs at least on a yearly basis.

• Dioceses say that they feel there are good priest/PLC relations in their dioceses.

• Dioceses feel that PLCs are effective in this sort of ministry.

• Dioceses feel that they have adequately prepared their parishes.

• Dioceses are pleased that parishes have remained open and functioning because of the PLC, that someone is in charge in these parishes without resident priests, that the parish has been empowered by the PLC and the PLCs are represented in diocesan functioning.

4. Areas of Challenge According to the Dioceses

• More dioceses should have plans for parishes without resident priests, as the lack of such plans has a negative impact on many areas of PLC and parish life.

• Dioceses face a number of push-pull factors in deciding on the use of PLCs.

• For those that espouse the PLC model, there has been a slowdown in adoption of this approach in recent years.

• At least from the parishioner's view, some dioceses may be installing PLCs in too precipitous a fashion or that they do so with insufficient communication. A sizeable number of parishioners do not feel that they have been adequately prepared.

• Certain features of the PLC contract need to be examined more carefully by some dioceses. Many PLCs feel that salary, benefits and contract length should be specified.

• To legitimize the role of the PLC and to give the incumbent more authority within the parish, more dioceses need to provide an installation ceremony for the PLC, preferably with the bishop present.

• More dioceses need to experiment with internships for PLCs, as the PLCs say this is the greatest omission in PLC appointments.

• While we collected no diocesan data to corroborate this point, the data from the PLCs indicate that some improvement needs to be made in relations with the deanery, diocesan officials and the bishop.

• More dioceses need to make some financial provisions for PLCs in poor rural or inner-city parishes.

• While a majority of dioceses do evaluate their PLCs at least yearly, 40 percent do not. Some room for expanded evaluation appears to be in order for some dioceses.

• Dioceses say that parishioners and diocesan priests are reluctant to accept this form of ministry, that there is a lack of sufficient parishioner education on the PLC role, that there is ambiguity in the PLC role and that the PLC's formation is inadequate.

5. What Is Working According to Parishioners with PLCs

• Sizeable majorities are willing to accept religious and deacons to be "pastors" of their parishes when no resident priest is available.

• Near majorities are willing to accept lay men, women and married couples as qualified to be "pastors" of their parishes when no resident priest is available.

• Parishioners who have experienced a PLC or several PLCs in their parish history are more willing to accept nonpriests as "pastors" of their parishes than those parishioners that have not experienced a PLC.

• Parishioners that have been without a resident priest in their parish are more inclined to accept nonpriests as "pastors" of their parishes.

• Parishioners overwhelmingly support their PLCs in their parishes and this support has grown through experience with the PLC in their parish.

• Most parishioners were open to the idea of a PLC coming to their parish and are even more open to the idea after working with them for a while.

• The experiences of living in a parish without a resident priest sometime in the past, of having one or more PLCs in their parish, of being open to having PLCs in their parish and believing that nonpriests are qualified to "pastor" their parish are conducive to parishioners' approval of certain nontraditional roles for the laity, to their taking a personal interest in these roles and to their willingness to train to become qualified for these roles.

• Eight to nine out of every ten parishioners studied gave very high evaluations of PLCs in all areas of their work.

• Parishioners who are open to the idea of a PLC in their parish, who support their PLC and who find non-priests qualified to "pastor" their parish are the most likely to give high evaluations to the work that the PLC is doing in their parish.

• Parishioners described many rewards in having a PLC in their parish, such as: she keeps the parish running smoothly, there is always someone to contact, she has personal contact with parishioners, there has been more awareness of parish needs, there is an increase in closeness with parishioners, people have been spurred by her leadership, the parish has more programs.

• Parishioners note that the relations between the PLC and the priests coming into the parish have been very good.

• Where parishes have teams, parishioners describe the relations between the PLC and the team as very good.

• The vast majority of parishioners envision that they will continue to have a PLC in their parish ten years from now.

6. Areas of Challenge According to Parishioners with PLCs

• Nearly 50 percent of parishioners with PLCs do not find a lay man or lay woman or a married couple qualified to "pastor" their parish in the event that the parish does not have a resident priest.

• Those most accepting of the nonpriest as a "pastor" may not be in the main stream of parish life, such as the divorced and remarried, the widowed, those not a member of the parish community.

• Those who have not experienced parish life without a resident priest and those who have not had PLCs are less likely to feel that nonpriests are qualified to "pastor" their parish in the event that the parish does not have a resident priest, are less likely to feel that certain nontraditional roles are appropriate for lay persons, are less interested in the roles themselves, and are less willing to undergo training to perform these roles.

• How parishioners learned they were getting a PLC was too often haphazard or informal—such as announced at Mass, told by the pastor to the parishioners or told by another parishioner—rather than the result of a discernment process.

• Parishes are too often selected for PLCs by a means other than a diocesan PLC plan, at least as perceived by parishioners.

• Nearly 50 percent of parishioners say that they had less than a month's notice that they were getting a PLC.

• Nearly 40 percent of parishioners felt unprepared by their diocese to accept a PLC. Parishioners feel that their dioceses should have prepared them in detail, explained the PLC duties better, sent a representative from the diocese for questions and answers, given longer notice, sent the bishop to talk with the parish.

7. What Is Working According to Parishioners Without PLCs

• When parishioners are aware that their diocese has a plan to remove their resident priest within five years or if they are aware of specific diocesan plans for multiparish priests, clusters, PLCs and teams in parishes, they are more inclined to say that nonpriests are qualified to pastor their parish and to have positive feelings about the eventuality of a part-time priest/PLC arrangement. In other words, the existence of diocesan plans for their parish helps them to accept alternate pastoring.

• About seven out of ten parishioners believe that the selection of a PLC for their parish, if it should happen some day, should be a joint decision of the parish and the diocese.

• Near majorities to substantial majorities of parishioners feel that eight specific nontraditional roles for lay persons are appropriate, are personally interested in these roles and would be willing to be trained when the following correlates are present: they believe their parish will be without a full-time resident priest in the future, are aware of a diocesan plan to appoint part-time priests in diocesan parishes and have positive feelings at the prospect of having a PLC in their parish.

8. Areas of Challenge According to Parishioners Without PLCs

• Two thirds of parishioners either believe they will be without a resident priest in the next five years or suspect that they may be without. Of those thinking they may lose their full-time priest even later, 70 percent are willing to entertain the thought that their parish may be without a resident priest at some future date.

• Nearly two thirds of these parishioners are not aware of any plans their diocese has to deal with parishes that will no longer have full-time resident priests. Likewise, they are unaware of any diocesan plans to reorganize parishes into clusters or to assign teams or PLCs to direct them.

• Majorities of these parishioners do not see lay men and women and married couples as qualified to "pastor" their parish in the event that they have no resident priest. Sizeable majorities do see deacons and religious as qualified, however.

• Majorities of parishioners tend to feel sad or unsatisfied at the prospect of a PLC coming to their parish in the event that they lose their resident priest. On the other hand their feelings of frustration, coldness or anger are likely to be only moderate.

F. Final Reflections

Our study has uncovered many interesting characteristics of the emerging ministry of the Parish Life Coordinator. We have discovered that there are many good things happening among the PLC's, dioceses, and parishes that we have investigated. Where dioceses encourage and support the ministry of the PLC, parishioners have a more accepting and open attitude toward the PLC.

However, not all aspects of the PLC model are perceived as positive, nor have all the difficulties been resolved to everyone's liking. One does get the sense that when things are going well between the PLC and the dioceses, relations with the parish are less positive.

We have not found any concerted evidence that parishioners are rejecting their PLCs. We have not even found a hypothetical rejection among parishioners who may have a PLC in the future. On the contrary, given time and encouragement by the diocese, parishioners are accepting the PLC model at high levels.

Within this general pattern of acceptance, PLCs dioceses, PLC's and parishioners find problems with the PLC and her ministry. We have strongly argued from our data that many of these difficulties could be reduced or alleviated if the broader church would better institutionalize the ministry of the PLC in its policy and planning operations. The relations of the PLC to all her associates, the level of ambiguity of the PLC's role, and the psychological well-being of the PLC would all likely become more positive if these formalization measures were enacted Parishioners would likewise be more open to having a PLC and accepting of their lay ministry responsibilities in the parish. These same parishioners would be more inclined to give their present PLC higher evaluations.

Our study, then, can be taken as evidence that the PLC model is generally accepted and working among the samples we studied. We are not at all sure that this level of acceptance means a bright future for the model. Our work has not touched upon the theological and ecclesiological dimensions of this phenomenon and it is in these areas that some find problems with this model of ministry. Our hope is that we have provided solid evidence to be used in the continuing debate over the merits and lack of merits of this emerging form of pastoral ministry.